EXPAT LIFE. NEW BEGINNINGS

by

G T DONNELLAN

GALLAN AMRAL

www.gallanamral.com

For Fionnuala & Brendan
&
Will, Klára, Siobhán, Liam, Niamh & Maxim

Dream big!

Also by the author

Fiction
The Greenway Conspiracy (paperback)
The Greenway Conspiracy (e-book)

Non-Fiction
Expat Life: New Beginnings (e-book)

Acknowledgements

THIS BOOK HAS been made possible, first and foremost, by the encouragement, support and example of my wonderful family: Martin, Fionnuala, Brendan, Will, Klára; and Siobhán, Liam, Niamh and Maxim; my siblings Frank, Michael, Carmel, Vincent and Myra and their families; and the Donnellan family: Tom, Mary, Noêlle and John and their families. Without Martin, my journey would have begun, and ended, in Ireland. I caught his dream first, then we dreamed together.

Special thanks go also to my global friends too numerous to mention; from those with whom I have an enduring and special friendship, to those whose ships tangented briefly with mine in the global village, and to the ones who come and go. My life is enriched because of you all. A special thank you to Tanya for sharing her writing journey, and her expat life with me, for encouraging me, picking me up when I stalled and pointing me back in the right direction, and for her Foreward to Expat Life: New Beginnings.

Special mention goes to the many contributors to Expat Life: New Beginnings. To Barbara, Sara, Ildiko, Martin, Fionnuala, Brendan, Becky, Ruth, Markku, Sue and Olapeju: your stories shine through these pages with individual messages for the reader.

And thanks to all, too numerous to mention, who walked alongside me, however briefly, on my expat journeys. You know who you are.

CONTENTS

FOREWARD

"Twenty years from now you will be more disappointed by the things that you didn't do than by the ones you did do. So throw off the bowlines. Sail away from the safe harbor. Catch the trade winds in your sails. Explore. Dream. Discover." – Mark Twain

PEOPLE LEAVE THE familiar shores of their 'home' for many different reasons. For some, it's to escape the pain, boredom, baggage or discomfort of the life they're living. For others, the reason centres on a new job, career, relationship, adventure or simply because their hearts desire is calling them to do so. Perhaps it's a combination of these motives. Regardless of the catalyst and "why's", beginning a new life in a foreign country and the practical elements involved in this overseas move will be similar .... accommodation needs to be sorted, perhaps a visa of some kind obtained, a new bank account, endless paperwork, packing and, possibly, arranging to store and/or sort through an old life of furniture and keepsakes. The practical components of what needs to be done prior to the move are mirrored in the settling in at the new location - redirect your mail, find a new address, sell some no-longer-wanted household goods, buy some more on arrival. These practical and tangible elements of a move are standard wherever you're headed - of course they can be extra challenging in a new country, and possibly a different language, but what needs to be done, remains the same. The logistics of a move are also over once they're done. There's a finish line! It's the emotional impact, the depth of personal growth and the reflection and redirection of becoming an expat that is often invisible and rarely discussed. Yet, no matter how many times you've done it before, the emotional impact of beginning a new life in another country is often the most important, challenging, treasured and long lasting outcome of a move overseas. Some of us thrive on change, for others it's an extremely difficult catapult into the unknown. Wherever you stand on this continuum, the emotional investment and influence of creating a life and community abroad can be far reaching and, sometimes, life changing.

This is why Geraldine has written the book she has. It is about a new beginning but most significantly it explores the mountains and valleys an international move can bring, along with the emotional impact on ourselves and those we care about, on our sense of home and where to next. From the initial decision, to the expectations of transition and the emotional considerations and support options throughout each phase of expat living, Geraldine, a seasoned expat herself, so gracefully and eloquently offers these insights, reassurances and learning opportunities. Through her own and ongoing experience of living abroad and the personal stories of those she's met along the way, she makes you feel that you are not alone in this journey we call expat living!

I met Geraldine and her husband on an expat journey of my own! One of the most treasured gifts of an overseas move can be the soulful, global and long-lasting connections that are made. This has certainly been the case in my friendship with Geraldine. My husband and I are honoured to be a part of her international family and cherished necklace of friends. Despite the physical distance of our subsequent moves, Geraldine's insight, compassion, wisdom and the perspective she continues to offer in all aspects of my life, including the gift and challenges of overseas living, remains unchanged. As an expert in expat living and all that entails, being consistently true to herself and all she continues to learn, we couldn't have a better teacher.

Let the journey begin ......

Tanya Dickson

Author[1], Teacher, Expat adventurer

---

[1] Her book, *Teaching Students with Learning Difficulties, why some people learn differently and effective strategies to help them,* is available from Amazon

PREFACE

More people than ever are living outside their home

culture:

'232 million international migrants living abroad

worldwide; 3.2% of the world's population,' UN global

migration statistics, Sept 11, 2013.

ARE YOU THINKING of moving to a different country to work - and live? Are you already in a new overseas post and looking for help or guidelines as to how to thrive in your new surroundings or deal with the emotional stuff it's throwing at you? Are you see-sawing between elation and depression in your new move? Are you beginning to think the price you are paying for living 'outside the box' is too high? Are you already thinking 'what next?'

Welcome to **Expat Life: New Beginnings**. This book is for expats everywhere but especially those contemplating putting their toe in the global waters for the first time. It explores the decision making processes of going or not going. It considers the issues with staying away or returning, and what to expect when you do. It sheds light on the newness of each move, the emotional stuff that sticks. It exposes the trials, tribulations and opportunities for families. It lays bare the dilemmas of social living in a way never before explored. And then it comes back to you. How are you now or, rather, who are you now? Where is it all going? Where will it all end?

DEFINITION OF TERMS

Throughout the book, the word '**expat**,' is used in the following way: an expat is a person who has left his or her home culture to work for a defined period of time in another culture. These expat journeys differ significantly from those of someone going on holiday. A person going on holiday has no intention of remaining indefinitely in the location; they bring sufficient funds with them for their time there; their actions are relaxation and fun based; and at the end of their allotted time they will return to their previous lifestyle to slot seamlessly back in to the work and living groove from which they escaped for a break. The expat, on the other hand, has burned the bridges behind him or her: they are looking to establish new work and living rules in a completely different culture, often amongst complete strangers.

There are exceptions to this, of course. History recounts tales of the Diaspora; whole cultural groups being disrupted and replanted in homogeneous groups in a completely different place. Large groups that stick together for survival reinforce their home culture; they are unlikely to adapt to local norms. In modern times, people who go abroad who use their own family groupings for support often experience a moderately similar state, e.g. the Irish abroad or the Czechs abroad. They live and work in a foreign country surrounded, and supported by, their own kind. Their experience of the new culture they find themselves in is measured by their immersion. Armed force bases outside the mainland experience something similar. These bases are designed to replicate the home-familiar but in a foreign place. It is possible for a person stationed in one of these bases to never leave the base; and if they do not, they are at home. There may be security regulations governing movement, of course. But often it comes down to the individual: do they want to explore outside the base or not. Similarly, with embassies and consulates worldwide; staff are posted for their ability to represent fully their nation to the host nation, to be on hand to assist their citizens if necessary. They have to be fully present in their home culture at all times; this is their specific job.

Culture is defined throughout simply as the diverse ways of living that people in different areas of the world have developed and enjoy. These differences emerge from millennia of survival and thriving in select family and extended groups, in select environments. Over time norms emerge regarding almost everything – from what to eat; how to eat; how to speak; how to look; how to marry; how to treat each other; how to govern; how to survive harsh climates; the list is endless. Groups isolated from each other develop different ways of speaking, the different languages we currently enjoy.

INTERNATIONAL MIGRATION STATISTICS 2013

Half of all international migrants live in 10 countries:

- United States 45.8 million
- Russian Federation 11 million
- Germany 9.8 million
- Saudi Arabia 9.1 million
- United Arab Emirates 7.8 million
- United Kingdom 7.8 million
- France 7.4 million
- Canada 7.3 million
- Australia 6.5 million
- Spain 6.5 million

MY EXPAT JOURNEYS

Since 1989 I have lived and worked as an international expat, most of the time alongside my husband, but occasionally on my own, and occasionally as a trailing spouse. The experiences, observations and advice in this book are gleaned from these years across Asia, Europe and Africa; and from many other expats, colleagues and friends along the way who shared their lives and stories with me.

Expat Life: New Beginnings was born of frustration at seeing countless individuals from varying nationalities experience similar difficulties in settling into their new environment, struggling through emotional responses that they had no answer to and felt they could not express. I have seen people grit their teeth, determined to portray a 'glass half full' mentality on the outside while on the inside the floor had dropped out of their world just when they had achieved their biggest dream. And the sadness was that most felt this was just them; just their own personal baggage, their own weaknesses. And so they kept quiet. I am talking here about the standard ups and downs of new culture living that are experienced uniquely; the disempowerment felt in new language situations; the jet lag; the sheer overload of new learning that has to take place in a short period when the most one wants to do is make a good impression at the exact time when a person is least best-equipped to do so. And the moments of emotional re-adjustment that hit out of the blue along the way, particularly in that first year. HR Departments do fantastic logistical jobs but they are not equipped to deliver emotional support. This is what this book is about. It is about what is under the hood; a commonality of experiences shared wherever you are in the world.

The similarities of life and work experiences are huge even though the personalities, and reasons for travelling to work, differ widely. This book defines these similarities to promote understanding of expat journeys; encourages through guidelines and examples; and promotes understanding between those who choose to go and those who choose to stay behind.

PART 1
TO GO OR NOT TO GO

"Some people live in cages with bars built from their own fears and doubts. Some people live in cages with bars built from other people's fears and doubts; their parents, their friends, their brothers and sisters, their families. Some people live in cages with bars built from the choices others made for them, the circumstances other people imposed on them. And some people break free."

C. JoyBell C.

1

PROLOGUE: TO GO OR NOT TO GO

IN THE WORLD of change there are two observable actions: you either move away from where you are, from that which is bothering you, that is not serving you well any more or you move towards something more attractive, something that will benefit you better. Although the outcome may be the same your state of mind will be different as you move forward depending on your starting point. The former relates to moving from a place of need; the latter, to a place of advancement. These first considerations are always personal; they are about you, which is absolutely correct.

The 5 P's

Five key words to keep at the forefront of your mind as you plan your move are:

1. **Perception**: you are viewing your world from a vantage point of 1 – you. Nobody else can fully understand what it is like to walk in your shoes. Other people have their own agenda, their own viewpoints. How are you seeing things? What are you expecting from the future? Is there a difference between the

way you see things and other people's viewpoints? And what value do you place on these other viewpoints? Are you being hot-headed? Stubborn? Or is yours the clearer vision?

2. **Purpose**: why are you doing this? Is there a better way? What do you want to achieve?

3. **Planicing:** are you planning or are you panicking or are you doing both at the same time? Can you slow things down to get a more complete picture? Is there someone you can get advice from? How fearful are you? Planicing always involves big doses of fear or anxiety.

4. **Performance**: can you actually move or are you daydreaming? What will you actually do when you get to your new destination? Who will you be then?

5. **Personality**: know your personality type and move with your strengths. As Steven Covey says in his book The 7 Successful Habits, what people see is personality, what is underneath is character. Give yourself a chance; know yourself as well as you can then be true to who you are.

You have one life. You owe it to yourself to live it to the best of your ability. **Part 1** provides insight and encouragement as you begin your journey to a new life. While it is written with the expat in mind, the form change takes is similar for anyone changing jobs locally or changing location inside their own country. What is really different for the expat is that change is done at a distance, often among complete strangers, and often in a foreign language.

> **Do or do not**
> **There is no try.**
> Master Yoda

2

MOVING AWAY

THE DECISION TO move away from where you are is a personal one.

> The thing is, whatever you are experiencing, you are not alone.

It is a choice. It can be anything from incredibly exciting to life shattering. And it is your choice as an adult to own. Sometimes these choices come easy; sometimes it takes a protracted process to prise us way. Sometimes the decision is presented to us in a way that is difficult to refuse; the consequences scream louder than the opportunities. And sometimes we are forced out by circumstances outside our control. As I write, someone somewhere is choosing to leave home or is being forced to. The thing is, whatever you are experiencing, you are not alone. While each of us processes experiences differently there is enough similarity for us to learn from, and be encouraged, in our life journey by our fellow-travellers. The expectation is that life will be better in this other place.

There are some key reasons for moving away:

- Money
- Survival
- Experience
- Escape
- Opportunity
- Adventure
- Wealth
- Natural disaster
- War
- Personal relationships
- Family
- Service
- Other – there's always other reasons that are deeply private that are rarely shared, and these often involve emotions.

MONEY is top of the list for those who are free to make a choice: money to pay bills; making money fast; money to get ahead; money to enjoy a better lifestyle; and money to travel more. It can drive people to live in inhospitable climates, environments, and culture; to work in hostile and unfriendly workplaces, and to live apart from loved ones and family. Often it is this living apart that can provide for a family. This area is full of contradictions. But it can also open the door on a new world, literally. There is nothing so amazing than proving to oneself that you can work in a new environment, amongst complete strangers, and enjoy it. The pursuit of money need not be an unpleasant experience at all. It can be wonderfully enriching once the stress of not having enough is replaced by the ability to pay one's way. Once you have enough, it is what you do with your money that makes the difference.

But what is enough? This is a complex question and one every person must answer for themselves. There are a few points that need mentioning directly to the expat who works for money:

1.   Once you get used to a good expat package it is difficult to even consider managing without. This can lead you to make poor choices about work conditions, locations or environments as you chase the better package. If you find yourself taking increasingly challenging jobs in increasingly difficult environments, ask yourself:

    a.   Does earning this amount of money = better lifestyle?

    b.   What lifestyle do I want anyway?

    c.   Is my money working for me or have I become a slave to money?

    d.   What's the end game here?

2.   Expat packages need to cover expenses that were not part of your home expense sheet. They may surprise and dismay you. Be forewarned. Two biggies are: travel 'home' and children's education. You will need to budget for airfares, where you will stay, car hire, meals out, shopping for familiar items of clothing and OTC[2] meds that may not be readily available where you now live. School fees are just the tip of the iceberg: consider uniform, books and materials, school meals, trips, to name the usual items.

3.   Whatever your money reasons for moving, once these are covered, acknowledge this and make new goals otherwise you run the risk of bringing the same money needs to each subsequent move. Create new, sustainable habits around the money you now have.

4.   Save money for relocation. I estimate you need a minimum of $5000 per person to move; $10,000 for a couple without children. I would suggest you add another $2000 per child.

---

[2] OTC Over the counter meds

Some companies offer great relocation packages and onsite support financially; others do little and you need to make sure you have enough with you for living plus all the other setups until you get your first pay cheque – apartment/house, internet, home goods, e.g. bedding, kitchen equipment, gym membership, social event money. Remember your shipment will not arrive with you; it usually takes 4 – 6 weeks and you will need to bring enough with you to get by until then.

5.   Save. This is really important to plan for. If you have moved to pay bills, your focus will naturally be on this, and rightly so. But if that is all you focus on, it is likely that in your next move you will have to borrow or realise money in some way to move, and the cycle happens all over again. I have seen many people with this repeat cycle. They get so busy with work that they do not make time to mark the moment when they realise their move's goal and set new goals.

I need to make another observation here. I am not advocating that you move to a new country, pay your bills and save the rest. Somewhere in here, I suggest you take some of that hard-earned money and explore your surroundings. Enjoy your new country and continent – if it is safe to do so. The old saying that 'travel expands the mind' is true; in fact, I would say it is permanently life-changing.

6.   Know what you are exchanging for the money you earn. Is it brains or brawn? Or both? Or is it your life-blood? There is a tendency in the expat work cycle to work 24/7; to be drawn into the unpleasant habit - and often the reason for the next move - of constantly working, constantly giving, in your newly adopted country and living or trying to have a life during holiday time.

For example, on one of our moves, my husband and I sat with the Chairman of the Board while he welcomed us to his country. In his smooth voice he informed us that he would pay us very well indeed but would suck us dry in the process. We laughed cordially. Who would do such a thing? Well, he did! He was entirely true to his words. The pay was amazing but we did nothing but work, work. This is what I meant by asking the question earlier about exchanging your life-blood for money. Consider carefully if it is really worth it in the long run.

SURVIVAL is a hard reason to live the expat life but there are more people doing this than you think so if you're one of them, you're not alone. To survive you need two initial things:

- Money. This old chestnut is everywhere. When I was a child it was drummed into me that 'the love of money is the root of all evil,'[3] and that 'it is harder for a rich man to enter heaven than a camel to get through the eye of a needle!'[4] But who does not long for money when they do not have any! There is neither dignity nor joy in being poor. If you do not have enough to eat or the bailiffs are coming to throw you out on the street, there will be nothing else on your mind but how to cover your responsibilities and put a decent meal on the table! There is nothing wrong in having money. There is nothing wrong in working your socks off to make money! It is all about what you do with abundance; how you live your life; how you treat those about you and the world in general.

When you are in survival mode, you are most likely to take any job overseas that will see you out of a pinch. Often the conditions are not good. This is ok. To use a car analogy, you have started the engine and pulled out from the kerb. The first kilometre is decided but the journey is far from over. Get going. Make the money you need to live, and when you are back in control of your life, start thinking outside the box. Look for the opportunities to improve your lot. Be prepared to learn.

---

[3] 1 Timothy 6:10
[4] Matthew 19:24

- A safe place to live. This is sometimes less considered when someone is in dire circumstances. Sometimes it does not even enter into the equation at all until you are standing at the airport or train station with a few coins in your pocket and not a clue which way to turn. This is where support groups are invaluable. If you are down on your luck, you will need someone to watch your back, to give you a safe haven until you get on your feet. Try and make this someone you know or can trust from a friend's recommendation.

If you are in the position to influence where you will stay initially be thorough in your research. Do not depend solely on the recommendation of your new HR Department. These are often staffed by local people who see the environment from a different point of view than you, and they see you differently. Expats are always presumed to have lots of money and you will most likely be directed accordingly. Ask what options are available. Ask about safety in the area. Ask about how long it will take you to get to work from there; how reliable the transport system is; how much it will cost. Ask these same questions from another expat if possible.

EXPERIENCE: Many people become expats in the first instance to gain valuable experience in their chosen job field that they cannot acquire for a variety of reasons at home. It may be because the learning is not available at home; the technological resources, the medical expertise. This move is about enriching personal skills, making the person more employable for the future. It is likely to be lower paid with longer hours and fewer benefits but the future gains outweigh these elements. But you have to keep these future gains at the forefront of your mind because human nature being what it is, it is easy to feel dumped on as this is a work situation where you really cannot say no. There is a time for building up personal skills, and a time for making money from them, for building a future.

That said, a new cultural living experience will impact you whether you are earning a packet or gaining experience - which equals a future packet. For some, this will impact deeply in your job field every second of the day; for others, more so when you leave work at the end of the day.

ESCAPE should never be a valid reason for living the expat life but unfortunately it is. I include here the person who constantly changes culture to escape from something inside themselves, a hidden enemy they are unable or unwilling to deal with; relatives and friends, and the wide swathe of the cast-offs left behind, would label him or her immature, selfish, and irresponsible. They often drift their whole life, happy in their unhappiness. Other 'escape' reasons are external even if their origins are complex and unclear; their solutions piecemeal, and very rarely easy or quick to find. These include:

- War or armed hostilities
- Family abuse
- Marital abuse
- Sectarian abuse
- Gender inequality
- Religious oppression
- Habit change
- Closed-minded communities

There is a tendency for expats to expect others to have moved abroad for a reason similar to theirs and undoubtedly, if that reason is money, you can be pretty sure that there is some element of that in every move. Maybe it rates 10/10 on the scale, or 3/10, but it is there somewhere. But expats who have moved for 'escape' reasons generally keep the reason to themselves unless it is the first or the last reason mentioned above. People who have moved for war or hostilities reasons have compelling stories to tell. They are lucky to be alive and they will celebrate that. People from closed-minded communities will be heard also. They seem never to tire of criticizing their past life environment, and there is a pattern here. Today's present environment will be tomorrow's past life experience. Often the criticizing continues in perpetuity. A wise person will realise there is no perfect environment: the only thing we can perfect is our response to the environment we choose to be in. Choosing to go is a choice; not going is a choice also whether this is unconscious or deliberate. I celebrate everyone's choice. If I don't, how can I acknowledge, own, and celebrate my own?

FAMILY ABUSE is terrible, being mistreated in your area of deepest trust and vulnerability a crime against humanity on the micro scale relative to war crimes on the macro. You are a survivor. What you seek in exile is a safe haven and anonymity as you build your desired life for the first time in complete personal freedom. It is most definitely a reason to go, to move away from your oppressors as fast as you can. Do not hesitate for a moment. Seek out help. Do it today.

MARITAL ABUSE is another reason to seek out a new life as an expat. Nobody deserves to be abused, to be put down, demeaned, emotionally deprived, beaten, or made to perform sexual acts against their will. Each one of us is a complete and worthy individual; absolutely none less than the other. Find someone who can help you today. Avail of personal counselling to build up your self-confidence. The victim image you have in your head is wrong. It was put there by someone who wanted to control you, to make you the person they want you to be. This is your time now. Who do you want to be?

SECTARIAN ABUSE is insidious. It is a blight on society. But while it reflects on the narrow-minded bully and the narrow-minded communities where it exists, it is the person who is the focus of the abuse that feels it most, often fearing for his or her life, or the lives of his or her family. The decisions to be made are fight it, flee from it or put up with it. I believe that everyone deserves the freedom to be themselves; to live in accordance with their beliefs in peace and prosperity. If it is your decision to flee the abuse, you will find many wonderful communities and countries prepared to let you live freely. Why should you settle for anything less?

GENDER INEQUALITY is a complex issue and one not easily fully resolved by an expat move. Some countries have decidedly unequal views about women; others more obviously equal but the glass ceiling for equality of the sexes in the workplace is still floating far above the heads of most women. In other areas, men are not welcomed as much as women in the workplace. Some activities are seen all over the world as best met by women; some by men. Some work areas are unashamedly biased. It takes a determined individual to breach the barriers. My experience internationally has been mostly favourable gender wise. The best person for the job got it usually - unless the boss is a Neanderthal and a complete sexist. And believe me, they do exist; both the male and female varieties. I have the scars to prove it!

But what is not always recognised is the role of personality type in gender equality. Men and women will be heard but not necessarily listened to equally. If you want to be listened to equally as a woman in the workplace have a good long look at yourself vis a viz your male counterpart. Ask yourself:

- Do I dress professionally? Does he? Chances are he wears a suit. Maybe he wears the same suit all the time, I hear you offer in disdain! It doesn't matter. He dresses for the job he wants. Do you?
- Do you draw attention to your feminine assets? How would you feel in a meeting if your male colleague wore a codpiece? It is possible to be feminine and neutral. Find the balance. You

have more leeway in a more gender mixed environment. Do you want your male colleagues to see you as a date or a serious challenge to their status quo? Give them something intellectual and professional to consider at work.

- Learn about the psychology of colour. While the rebel inside you may well want to wear bright pink to liven up the black suits, consider the impact. You, as a person, are more likely to be a focus of attention rather than the expertise you bring to the table. Keep the pink until you're the boss!

- As a woman, consider the timbre of your voice. Is it high-pitched? Nasal perhaps? Or soft spoken, difficult to hear? Or just plain loud? Observe the general tones at meetings. Observe the responses or reactions that arise from your tone of voice. A short session of voice training can help you adjust to a profile that means success.

These are just a few things to get you started. Of course, you may totally disagree with me, and be up in arms with me about this approach. We are what we are surely. No - we are what we plan to be! Equality is a professional choice that starts in your head. Men all over the world are born to believe in themselves. Women are too! What happened to us along the way is somebody else's life lessons.

My community upbringing instilled in me the visible profile of the male dominated society where the man brought home the money and the woman's work was to support her man. I knew I was as smart and as valuable as my male siblings and set out to prove my worth. It was an uphill battle. When I worked in IT I decided to shorten my name to Gerry which worked a treat. It sounded male and until I turned up to lead meetings, new contacts didn't know any better. Ten years ago, getting people in the room as a female IT trainer was the main work. I knew if they were there I could keep them there. But the sad truth was that the gender bashing I got was from other women! Society still has a long way to go to free the minds of women from the yoke of misplaced work-appropriate options. Most men have moved on. Why can't we, as women?

RELIGIOUS OR STATE OPPRESSION is a more virulent form of sectarian abuse. It holds a whole country in its grip, not just key elements inside select communities. It contains many difficult elements but one in particular is very distressing. It is the element of informant spying: the watched society. People are encouraged to inform on other's misdemeanours for the privilege of being called model citizens. The people informed on are part of the informer's local village, as it were; often they are family members. It breeds mistrust and deep feelings of betrayal. People often flee for their lives to a new country, to live as expats for the rest of their lives.

But this freedom is bitter-sweet. You leave family behind who may be persecuted in your absence. Your family may have no choice but to disown you. Maybe they were the ones to inform on you to preserve their own freedom, their own way of life. Either way, your expat experience is likely to be personally painful and lonely initially. You have paid a high price for your freedom. But you are free! Hang onto that lifeline!

HABIT CHANGE is a common reason, but not usually acknowledged openly, for leaving where you are to experience the expat life. The expat life is seen as a new opportunity, in a new environment, to escape destructive habits and create the life you truly want. The new environment is the key here. As an expat, you are free to create a new life. You put yourself in a position where you can make different responses to old pressures should they re-emerge. Chances are they will. Chances are you will make different, more positive choices this time around. What negative environmental pressures could you possibly be experiencing that moving overseas will release you from?

- Drugs. I have observed drug users who wish to free themselves from habitual use, do so, by moving to a completely different cultural environment. If drug use is not a normal part of the new environment, or as readily available, it aids the withdrawal from habit. Additionally, with moving abroad your focus is moved outward. You have new challenges that keep you occupied. And you have no supplier yanking your chain day and night.

- Alcohol. Ease of availability is a key factor in the overuse of alcohol in societies. While not a solution in itself for the alcoholic, it does make keeping sober a whole lot easier if there is none available socially!

- Smoking. Moving from a situation where smoking is popular and endemic to one where its use is frowned upon and banned will certainly be a boost to the person whose desire is to quit. It is easier to find identification groups to align with; there are many! Seeing how others in different cultures deal with their issues without smoking is helpful and illuminative. You may even identify that the issues that caused you to smoke were environmentally dependent anyway.

- Low self-confidence. This is a negative, destructive, inaccurate, self-perpetuating habit, and there are many who will be happy to keep you in this mould. The very act of moving overseas as an expat or even thinking about the possibility breaks the cycle. If you can take one step, you can take two. Overseas, you are looked on as brave and adventurous, and so you are!

If you have escaped to a better place where you are free to make the decisions and choices for yourself, I congratulate you! You have one chance in this life to be all that you can be. Make it a good one! Reach for the stars! You belong there, like everyone else.

If for some reason you find yourself reading these words from a place that is restricting your growth, from stopping you from being all that you can be, seek help today or at the very least, begin to look. That is your starting point. You can do that. Everyone can do that.

OPPORTUNITY is a very different reason to become an expat than the ones previously discussed. It presents as a true choice. There you are, working away happily in a job you love with your life in order and opportunity knocks. This can be in the form of a promotion within your firm or an invitation to join another or the job you have always wanted is advertised. Either way, this is the first time you have to consider what you stand to lose as well as what you stand to gain. You find yourself in an enviable and unenviable situation simultaneously. What to do? Do you go with your heart? Do you make exhaustive long comparison lists? Do you involve others in your decision or not? Do you face up to the challenge immediately or keep putting it off waiting for divine inspiration? It all depends on who you are and ultimately what secretly pulls your strings.

But the free choice opportunity provides often comes with hidden costs and issues attached. Consider the promotion within your firm that you have ached after - but it is in Brazil. Can you afford to say no? Is your job security on the line if you choose not to go? Probably. Can you keep your family together if you go? Maybe. Will your partner wait for you or join you? Again, maybe. What about your children? How will they fare? And your aging parents? And your friends? Pure opportunities carry a heavy decision load around people as opposed to money. I suggest this can be as high as 10/10 for some people. There is no right or wrong here; only choices. I suggest you make your lists. Talk to people who matter. Do it straight up. Do not leave it until the last moment because you will only go with your gut at this stage. But in the end, that is exactly what you do. Go with your gut, your intuition, for no one can read the future perfectly. But better an informed gut than a hasty decision. I think deep down a person knows what is best for them. You just need the time to consider what is best for everyone. Once you make the decision, do not look back! Move forward with expectation into your new life. One of the nice elements of opportunity is that it truly gives you the chance to create your own life, or at least have a decent say in what you will be experiencing for the coming few years. How wonderful is that!

30 year old Ruth Waters writes:

I left Liverpool, UK in August 2013 to move to Shanghai, China. I had only ever been on short holidays with friends before this and so was prepared for the worst when I decided to not only move over 7,500 miles across the globe but go and live in a country where both culture and environment are vastly different than what I was used to.

Before I left, I was told by friends and family alike that I would experience a honeymoon period and then a state of panic and doubt where I'd want to go back home. I waited and waited for that "moment" many people spoke of but honestly, the honeymoon period has never left me! I wake up every morning with the biggest smile on my face and count my blessings at the life I have.

There are things that I miss about England but that's the sacrifice you make. It's only the material things I miss in England because technology makes contact with friends and family almost too easy! It makes those trips back home at Christmas and the summer that extra bit special now because I have stories and experiences to share that have enhanced me physically, mentally and spiritually. No amount of money can buy that kind of experience! My career is progressing in ways I never thought possible and look forward to every day optimistically and enthusiastically.

I would recommend anyone with even 1% curiosity of travelling to throw caution to the wind and do it. I guarantee in twenty years, when you look back you will not regret doing it, you'd only regret not doing it.

ADVENTURE is often spoken about as the starting point for expat living for the perceived lucky few but in reality it is a mindset that is available to all. We all have the opportunity to view life's choices or journeys as adventures or struggles. All adventures contain an element of struggle, of pushing past your comfort zone, to realise a dream, goal or objective. All struggles contain the opportunity to see beyond the obvious; moments of being fully present when a bird bursts into song beside you or a flower you have never seen before captures your attention by its beauty or fragrance – a moment of transportation out of drudgery that points to a surrounding that holds more than you have appreciated. Who knows where this new vision will lead? Who knows the tipping point when an adventure becomes a drudge, or worse still, a nightmare?

But having spare money enters into the concept of adventure too. So does discretionary available time, and it is best if these two elements converge at the same time! You need money, or a similar catalyst of some sort, to propel you to a physical place, or a mental construct, so the adventure may begin. The implication here is that the more money you have, the more adventures you can experience as it is likely, with this money, you will have the additional time at your disposal. Why then do we observe wealthy people living what the adventurer describes as mundane lives? Boring. Parochial. It comes back to choices. People make the best choices based on the information they have at the time. It is the quality of this information that changes how people see the world; plus the permission they feel they can give themselves to experience it.

WEALTH is an interesting thing to chase as an expat. You have got past working to live and now you have the chance to create a lifestyle you enjoy. Wealth is abundance in all things positive - money, time, property, art, health, travel, whatever you want or need to enjoy. There is no waiting for something; it is available now. You can experience the best life has to offer as a global citizen. Somehow the word 'expat' does not quite fit anymore. You can be global at the flick of a switch with wealth. You can fly out of a country as quickly as you flew in, if you want. An expat usually has to fulfil a contract; has some agreed time limit in situ. Sometimes you are born into wealth; sometimes you work your own way into it. There is no right or wrong, only choices made along the way. Using your wealth well can be immeasurably enriching for all. Your energy and money will follow your focus. You have a chance to make a real impact for good in societies worldwide.

But does having a lot of money, and flitting in and out of places at will, really make you a global citizen? Some would argue yes, some no; and I believe it all revolves around what elements you include in the definition of citizenship. A citizen has an unalienable right to live in society: this is conferred by birth or by law. A citizen has rights under the laws of this society; sometimes these are defended vigorously, often they just provide the landscape background against which society functions. But a citizen also has responsibilities as how one then lives; and how one lives surpasses the function of laws and moves towards the esoteric and spiritual. Surpassing the law is what enriches a culture; it is the value-added individuals bring to society; the yeast that leavens the whole dough. And just as yeast takes time to work, so a person needs time for their personal magic to benefit society. At the very least, a person wishing to adopt the term 'global citizen' should consider what sustainable value they bring to the societies they interact with; what respect they diffuse with their actions; what legacy they leave behind.

NATURAL DISASTERS are particularly traumatic reasons for living as an expat though this feels more like living as an exile. The place you called home has risen up against you and thrown you out unceremoniously and instantly. All the hard work you have put in throughout your life is gone. Every single thing you own is gone. Sometimes your family are gone too. All you possess is you, just as the day you were born, but worse. As a baby, you had a natural support group. You were expected to be dependent. But as an adult, you have experienced the satisfaction of self-sufficiency and self-reliance. It can be very hard to accept help at the very moment you need it most - that is, if you are lucky enough to have help available. You can only look forward when you most want to dream about what you once had. The change moment was catastrophically quick. You now have a stark choice. Stay and rebuild, and chance going through all this again in an uncertain future, or start again in another country, if you can. This is a survival choice initially. There is no right or wrong choices, only best fits.

There is a slow-burning natural disaster that causes migration too; a product of industrialisation. It is air pollution, measured by the AQI (Air Quality Index). High AQI readings can be deal-breakers for expats and locals. Many expats over the age of 50 will have memories of air-pollution in their home countries, when they were young, if they lived in a major city or industrial belt. I have memories of this myself living in Dublin in the early 1980s. The city burned coal to keep warm and there were many days in the winter of 1984, before my husband and I left for the UK, when the smog never lifted. Then the government intervened with incentives to upgrade to oil and smoke free central heating and the problem gradually reduced. At the time of writing this I was living as an expat in a city of more than 24 million where the AQI is alarmingly high in winter, and while solutions are being sought and measures implemented, it will take years to make the air safe all year round. This was a deal-breaker. Way back in the 1980s, I did not believe I had an option for change. I believed I just had to make do; manage the air pollution as best I could. Today, the danger to my health outweighs the benefits I perceive I am in receipt of. This is my choice. New people arrive every day, and others stay for decades. People view things differently and will make up their own minds. Recognising available choices is the beginning of personal freedom.

WAR, or civil unrest, is another traumatic reason for living as an expat. Your home may still exist physically but it has now become too dangerous a place to stay. It is likely that any expat life choices initially are seen as temporary, until the hostilities subside, and you can go home and rebuild. I speak here of individual choices to escape the conflict zone rather than mass refugee exodus. On mass, refugees neither seek nor desire to live as expats in another land. They simply want a safe haven until they can return home. In natural disaster situations, the enemy is the natural world; in war situations the enemy is other people so the element of right and wrong is present. It is possible to fight, to organise protests against other people, to right a wrong. That produces an additional element of choice that follows a new war-expat: redress. It is like standing with a foot in each life, each country, and each culture. Every life decision has to take into account a variety of 'home' situations. It is compromise living. Who knows what the outcome will be.

PERSONAL RELATIONSHIPS are very high on the list when considering leaving or staying whether from a home situation or an overseas position. This is a difficult area. Separation and heartache make poor companions on the journey of a lifetime. And there is nothing like an overseas move to reveal personal insecurities and perceived inadequacies. A move together has to work for both or serious cracks will show in the relationship within a very short time. Being together abroad can be too high a price to pay regardless of the beauty of the environment or all that extra disposable income. It is important that both commit to the move; to be 'glass half-full' people if this is to work well. I separate out the terms 'romantic interest', 'partner' and 'spouse' purposefully because of legal regulations in some countries only. This is your first stop in investigating a 'together' move. Who can you legally bring along? Countries differ. Make sure you understand fully who can accompany you.

I see three possible challenges here that generate many friction points:

- Romantic interests may be just that regardless of where you are in the world. So if you have accompanied your boyfriend or girlfriend overseas and your relationship flounders, what will you do? Do you have enough money to return home independently? Will your qualifications be recognised in this new country so you can legally seek work in your own right?
- You are in a serious, committed relationship with your partner of many years and the country you are seeking to live in will not recognise this legally. What will you do?
- Your spouse really does not want to leave home and begin all over again. What will you do? Or he or she comes with you but you are working 16 hours a day? How will you both deal with this? Has she or he given up a successful career to sit and wait upon you in another country? Believe me, from what I have seen and experienced, no additional amount of disposable income or wealth will make up for this! You had better have a rock solid relationship! And you had better plan time together every week too! I have seen too many distressful relationship situations develop this way. This is where the opportunity of a lifetime can become hell on earth! Plan, and plan some more TOGETHER.

FAMILY is without doubt the most considered part of any move, and so it should be! Initially I define family as parents with children wishing to move. The impact on their lives cannot be overestimated whether a parent moves alone to work or the whole family moves. This is another list making situation; another talk to the experts situation. And most definitely a talk together situation, openly and frankly, not just once but many, many times. I suggest you go somewhere as a couple to do this, like, go have a coffee. Yes, I said coffee! When discussing finances and emotions, which will be high on the agenda, if you begin drinking alcohol it can cloud your reasoning, it is easy to overdo it, and old grievances can emerge and get tacked onto the current discussion. This is a time to be decidedly clear headed. Take the discussion outside your home comfort zone. Avoid discussing the move in the areas you find solace and rest. The last thing you want is to end up having an argument in bed! And once you have reached an inner peace and agreement around the situation then involve your children. But discuss the move with your children at home, if possible. They need to be able to retreat to their haven, their comfort zone, to mull things over or simply to cope with the shock you have just delivered them. Give them their space and be frank with them when they ask questions. It is amazing where children of all ages can express when faced with such a family move. If you are normally a 'glass half-full' couple, outward looking and adventurous, it is likely your children will have caught some of this from you. But I have observed that as with adults, some children need a physical anchor in the world, others are happy with the status quo of wherever you are. Be sensitive to this when dissolving assets. Be sensitive also to the fact that children will grieve for their friends and extended family. It is a tough thing you ask. I have seen family moves being successful time and again. Moving cultures is a wonderful learning ground for all. And now you will have the money to make the most of it!

There is another aspect to 'family' that I would like to explore here: the leaving the family nest for the first time. It is healthy to leave home, to set out by yourself, to take the freedom to think in your own head, to own your thoughts, have the freedom to act on them and the maturity to accept responsibility for your actions. It is a necessary part of growing up. Healthy family relationships will recognise this and encourage and support your efforts. But it is also a natural part of life for parents to want to keep you around. After all, they love you and enjoy your company. It is not unusual for one parent or the other to fall into the habit of living vicariously through you. You have so much more going for you than they ever did. And they are only human; they are fallible. They make the best decisions they can with the information they have. This is normal family behaviour although it can feel like emotional blackmail. Be gentle but firm. This is your time, your life. You can go gently and keep communication open. You may still be drawing financial support from your parents or family. There will be plenty of time to give back in the future.

I am often asked the question, 'Why am I the only one in my family that has left to live as an expat?' This is regularly asked in frustration; sometimes in wonder. There is no set answer to this question that works for everyone but there are some genetic comparisons observed with the incidence of alcoholism. It was initially proposed that if either parents were alcoholics, it was likely that the offspring would exhibit alcoholic tendencies too, a particular gene being identified as being switched on resulting in the inability of the person to control one's drinking once one had started; in other words, alcoholic parent = alcoholic offspring. It was predetermined; no personal element of choice was in play. We now know this is incorrect. An alcoholic parent or parents simply predisposes offspring to this outcome, by example as much as gene, but choice can, and does, intervene. There are many children of alcoholic parents out there who are not alcoholics; and there are many children of non-alcoholics who are alcoholics. Other factors are in play. A similar observation is made with expat living. It is suggested that if a parent or a grandparent lived and worked outside their culture, it was likely that a travel gene had been switched on and that this predisposes offspring to leave home and live as an expat in their turn. But, as in the state of alcoholism, a choice is observed. It may be an easy choice as it seems impossible to stay. It is as if the family mould is too restrictive for the talents of the individual who chooses to go. They need a bigger canvas to paint their life experiences on. And what about those who stay? Do they not have the same gene, if it exists? I have no answer for this. I am the only one in my family that has lived outside my home-culture all my adult life. My grandfather and grandmother emigrated to the US and became US citizens before returning home individually to an arranged marriage. My father worked for seasons in another country. My three brothers did short stints abroad too before calling it a day and settling to live in close vicinity to the rest of the family. On my husband's side, he is the only one in his family to live his entire adult life abroad. He is the eldest; I am the youngest. His grandfather emigrated to the US also, returning home late in life to an arranged marriage also. In the end, life expectations play a major part in feeding the choice to leave or to stay.

SERVICE to country and God are deep personal reasons to live life away from your home culture for short or long periods. This may be as a posting in the military, diplomatic service, Peace Corps, or church mission. There are particular circumstances surrounding these postings that are dealt with more comprehensively in **Expat Life: Carousel Moves**

OTHER: There are so many individual reasons, both simple and complex, why people move to work and live in another culture that it is impossible to cover all of them in this book. Here is a smattering of these real choices people have made along the way. I have not authored these to protect anonymity.

"I left to get away from my sister. She was driving me mad she was so bossy!"

"The new boss is a pig. He has it in for me. Better to go before I lose it!"

"I felt stifled at home. Every year the opportunity margin diminished. I would look longingly at the cars on the highway and wonder when my time would come."

"I woke up one morning and had a look around. It suddenly dawned on me that if I stayed I'd end up exactly like them. There was nothing wrong with them. I just wanted something more for me."

"I always wanted to travel. My dad would read me bedtime stories of far away and I would close my eyes and picture myself in the story. For a long time I didn't know how to begin, how I could leave my family. But my mum sorted that out for me. She just said, 'Go out there and make something of yourself. Don't be waiting around here for handouts!'"

"My decision to leave and never go back was simple. If I didn't go, I feared for my life! I was so scared!"

"I escaped from my drug habit; I left it behind me. It was the only way. I was out of control and in danger of losing everything I'd worked for. In the end, there was no place to hide, no place to escape to that didn't contain memories to keep me in the loop. My new best buddies were other addicts. I was scared shitless!"

"I left to make my fortune. It's that simple. There was nothing going for me at home."

"I wanted to make enough money to buy a fast car and impress the girls."

"I saw them making a match for me and I had to get out of there fast!"

"I had a fascination with Asian culture. Where it came from, I don't know. I badly wanted to live there for a while."

KEY EMOTIONS

To go or not to go is a choice. The decision is yours. There is no right or wrong decision only the one that best fits your situation. There are a few emotions that feature highly in the decision process that you need to be aware of:

- Fear is a high ranking guest at every decision table. It is often the most loquacious one; and the one most likely to have the final say. It masquerades as your voice of reason.
- Anxiety is Fear's lesser cousin but is more pervasive. It becomes your shadow. It nags and wears you down.
- Excitement sits on the other side of you from fear. It has a strong, melodious voice, pleasing to the ear. You listen to it by choice until Fear and Anxiety crowd it out. It is the voice of the future; a chime ringing in the unknown. It chases Fear around your insides. Which one has the bigger presence in your life? It is the one you give the most attention to.
- A persistent feel-good factor about a proposed move is often enough to seal the deal. It needs to be strong enough to push Anxiety aside and quiet the excesses of Fear and Excitement. Finally, you're able to sleep well again!

To go or not to go involves a decision process around many factors some of which are crystal clear, some foggy. The logistics of going or staying are the easy part; emerging from beneath the emotional family and social canopy the hardest. People live in the shelter of each other. Often our unconscious leads the way and our heart beats to this unidentifiable drum making the best decision we can with the information we have to hand and can manage. Sometimes the decision is cemented for us by unforeseen circumstances and we can feel caged in or thrown out. Often we feel we have to go against the grain in the pursuit of our dream leaving pain in our wake and in our heart. But whatever we decide, there is no right or wrong, only best fit. Sometimes this best fit spins so tightly around our person that it is all about me/myself; sometimes the best fit spin includes significant others. Often our decisions are hijacked by others who make our move all about them. You will find both positivity and negativity around your decision. Your personal power lies in your moment of choice. There are no doors shut against you except the ones you have consciously closed yourself or those you have yet to push against to see what happens. Whether you decide to go or to stay I honour your decision. Take control of your life and step into the future with confidence.

3

THE JOURNEY BEGINS

CONGRATULATIONS! YOU'VE made the decision to go! The contract, or not, has been signed – you might be going 'blind' without a job lined up - and you're ready for go, but not just yet, usually. You have to wait some time:

- To work out your notice to give your boss enough time to find a suitable replacement for you
- For the processing of a work visa, police checks if you work with children, and the translation and verification of documents, if applicable.

In the end, you find yourself with a foot in each world for an indefinite period of time and this can be both overwhelming and underwhelming alternatively or simultaneously. It also gives those in your close orbit, and not-so-close, time to advise you. Be prepared. Not everyone will view your decision positively. And the closer you get to your departure date, the more emotional the move may become. There are three main areas you might expect to grapple with during this period:

- Personal feelings
- The responses of others
- Logistics

PERSONAL FEELINGS

You have done it! You have created the next step in your life. It is an amazing feeling; in fact, this can feel so good it can become addictive! You have pushed the door open. You are on your way. You have been externally validated. Someone out there recognises your worth. It is a heady moment. Enjoy the rush. Immerse yourself in it. The fantastic news is that no one can take this away from you - that is, unless you give them permission to. It is all yours! You have earned it!

You begin to dream, right there and then. You picture yourself in the new environment. Your even feel the excitement and early anxiety in your stomach. You want to decide where you will stay; what kind of transport you will use, what food you are going to enjoy, who you might meet. If a foreign language is involved, you might invest in language classes or a good DVD. But first of all, you want to celebrate, tell others of your success. You are on top of the world!

Choose carefully whom you first share your news with. Make sure it is someone who will support you wholeheartedly, someone you can return to to be affirmed again. Not everyone will see your news as the best thing ever! Everyone filters news through their own experiences and expectations; most through the emotional filters of fear and loss first. It is a sad fact that many dreams are shot down by those nearest and dearest in the first telling – and not always by words alone. Withdrawal behaviour from others at this stage is very painful to deal with: try and understand that this is their issue, not yours. Your decision to leave has broken the pattern of life and they will need time to work out how they will adjust to your absence. The good news is that there are as many who will be thrilled for you, as not. You do not need an army of positive support behind you; one will do, and that can be someone you are moving towards, a positive stranger even.

Over the next few weeks, it is possible that you will be pulled back from your decision. Friends are more attentive than before, family loving and caring; even the work you are looking to change, or the work environment, seems idyllic. This is all normal; expect it. You are now viewing your current situation from the vantage point of the new location, the new job; and the familiar is comforting. Your friends, family, and work associates ARE treating you differently. You are leaving, so they are making the best of the remaining time they have with you. This is not the time for silly arguments or long lasting feuds. You begin to wonder if you have made a huge mistake! You swing between pleasure and happiness in the current situation, and increased anxiety and reduced excitement for the one to come. Underlying all this may be a niggling annoyance at others. Why could they not have behaved like this earlier then you might never have sought to move? Stop right there! This is not about others; it is about you. You have the right as an adult, and the obligation to yourself, to be the decider in your own head. You get to live your life, your way. You get to make your own mistakes and grow as a person as you accept the consequences. Now is the moment to bring back to memory the initial feeling of euphoria when you were offered and accepted the new job, when you cemented the new direction your life would take. Also remind yourself why you wanted to move in the first place.

Expect to feel:
- Excited
- Happy
- Joyful
- Anxious
- Fearful
- Angry

- Annoyed
- Reluctant
- Stubborn
- Mean
- Put-upon
- Had
- Manoeuvred
- Light-headed
- Tight-fisted
- Irresponsible
- Childish
- Powerful

This list is not meant to be exhaustive, only indicative. Add your own items. And remember, you can experience some of these, none of these, some all the time, some simultaneously, some daily, weekly or minute to minute. I have yet to meet an expat who does not relate to this list in some way or other. And I have yet to meet an expat who offers that they do. Yet when asked, they will acknowledge they have. It is as if there is some secret code out there that dictates such feelings could not be part of any considered international move. And I meet individuals who are confused, and feel bad, that in the midst of their dream move such feelings exist at all. Now, let the truth emerge once and for all. Change engenders feelings of challenge and insecurity; both negative and positive feelings emerge as a consequence. We all feel them. The greater the perceived challenge is, the wider the range of feelings, and their intensity, that we experience. Expats often keep quiet about these in case they put themselves in a position to be enticed back into the comfort zone; they just see them as a consequence of their choice. When you feel overwhelmed, take three

> Change engenders feelings of challenge and insecurity; both negative and positive feelings emerge as a consequence.

deep breaths into your abdomen, and reaffirm you chosen journey and what it will mean to you in the long run. This is useful at night too when you cannot sleep, when your mind is buzzing with possibilities and shows no sign of slowing down.

OTHERS RESPONSES

While you have the power and ability to control your own response to the new move, you have absolutely none over others' responses. Prepare for a roller coaster experience. You are about to experience the highs and lows of interpersonal relationships at an intensity level that is normally reserved for breakups! Well, you are, after all, breaking up - from whole communities at the same time!

Depending on the amount of notice you have to provide, and the calibre of the workplace, you may be in for a pleasant or a torrid few months. Usually there are elements of both. The ones that most people mention first are the negative experiences; these have to be managed carefully:

- Sarcastic comments about you considering yourself a cut above your colleagues
- Deprecating comments regarding you leaving them in the lurch
- Cold-shoulder behaviour excluding you from any meaningful involvement in decision making from then on
- Dumping behaviour requiring you to punch above your weight so they can get the very most out of you in the remaining time
- Jealous jibes at your expense slighting your professionalism which translates into 'lack of professionalism'.

Despite the fact that you are leaving and may not want to rock the boat, you need to address any attack on your professionalism and challenge exclusion from forward decision making in your area. You are there to give your best until the second the clock stops. If they do not want your continued input, that is their choice, but you have flagged the inconsistency and affirmed your commitment to the end. You can leave with a clear mind, and it will be noted where you may least expect it.

On the pleasant side, people will:

- Affirm your decision, congratulating you on moving onwards, and upwards, if that is your choice
- Admire your courage openly. A lovely side-effect from your decision is that others will emulate you; you become their hero. It is as if by you stepping outside the box of the ordinary, you have given others permission to follow or at least, you have shown them the way.
- Offer to help logistically
- Offer contact help in your new country
- Be a support group in the background, countering the negativity where it occurs, to ensure your remaining experiences are pleasant and worthwhile.

Hold onto these contacts. Be thankful. It is positive people like these that make living each day a happy challenge.

Here are some representational comments I've come across in my travels:

- "You're going to Prague! Fantastic! I'm first in line for the spare room!"
- "You're going where? Tokyo? So what have they got there that we don't?"
- "If you leave, if you go out that door, that's it! Don't ever return!"
- "So, you're off then? Lucky for some! I guess I'll be still alive when you get back."

- "Aw, Geraldine! Don't go. It's so far away! What'll we do without you? We'll never see you anymore!"
- "So, what are we going to do with this system you've installed? We spent all this money on it for you. Who will run it now?"

When you put these comments, and any like them, with the tears and silences, the cold shoulder, the false bravados, the personal blame, the letting down, it is a wonder folk ever go anywhere! But putting it all in perspective, what people are saying badly is how much they appreciate you and how much they will miss you. They are also edgy that you are moving outside their control, and perhaps even jealous that you are moving onwards while they perceive they cannot. While it is fine for you to redefine your life, by your choice, others have now to deal with change they would rather not have to, and it is your fault. The emphasis subtly changes from it being all about you to being all about them. Try and see people's responses for what they are and stay close to your true friends. If necessary, challenge the new status quo. Tell people clearly, as often as is necessary, that the move is about you, and your choices. How they respond is up to them.

The above paints a bleak picture, a representational one, but it is not the only one. If you are fortunate enough to be in a positive family dynamic, a progressive work environment, and a supportive friends' community, you will have the backup you need. Your move will be smooth; your initial enthusiasm unhindered. There are gender considerations here also. Generally, I have observed less 'home' issues with men changing cultures than women. For all advances in equality, there is still a deep feeling that women need more support than men, that they are more vulnerable from predators, and more inclined to feel upset about 'leaving'. While the vision of a man walking away from his wife and crying children pulls at the heartstrings, it is still entirely different if the picture changes and it is the woman who is walking away from the husband and crying children. The sense of outrage, regardless of economics, is huge. On the other hand, the silence is deafening if same-sex partners inhabit the same picture. Why? I suggest it is because society has not worked out the rules yet for these relationships as it has for heterosexual couples so there is no mass response. I wonder who society feels sorry for: the man, the woman or the children. In the end, you have to be strong enough to weather any storm society throws at you in the pursuit of your dream. If you are not, you will always be at someone's beck and call. You may like to be at someone's beck and call but make sure it is an active choice not a consequence of inaction.

LOGISTICS

Every move requires some reorganisation of personal assets. You may have a lot or you may have few possessions but you will still need to work out what you want to take with you and what you want to leave behind. There are many excellent logistics companies who will advise you and transport your goods for you once you have decided what to do.

There are a number of different ways you can approach your move;

1. Take everything with you. This is a model I see many people with children adopt. It provides complete home-from-home familiarity which can ease the settling in period significantly. You will have a few weeks delay as you wait for your new residency to be completed before taking delivery of your shipment but this can be explained away as holiday time.

Additionally, this can save a lot of money and inconvenience as you have your usual, familiar items for the bedrooms and kitchen, in particular. You avoid the build-up of several sets of saucepans and multiples of electronic goods. And some goods are simply not available in the area you are transferring to. Conversely, it is expensive to ship your stuff all over the world, time and again. There is a danger that you ship rubbish, stuff you should have thrown out, items you will never use in another climate. And white goods[5] do not ship well. And you will need to consider step-down or step-up transformers when changing regions.

2. Take nothing with you apart from the clothes on your back and a suitcase. This is a very freeing state to be able to move about in but it is not often practicable. Consider the following:

   a. How tall are you? Will you be able to purchase clothes your size in your new location? Or shoes? Or underwear? Chances are you will, but is the cost manageable? You might be able to buy in only one store, and these exclusive stores are expensive. I am 5'8" and take a 41 shoe size, and when I moved to Tokyo I had real difficulty finding somewhere to purchase new clothes and shoes. I started a trend then which continues until today – I buy most of my clothes when I visit home. I continued this practice when working in Lagos. In Shanghai, I got clothes copied really well. On the other hand, my husband is 5'7" and wears a size 42 shoe size. He is able to purchase clothes and shoes to fit everywhere, at regular prices.

During vacations I travel out with a near empty suitcase that I plan to fill with necessary clothes for the coming year. I wander around my familiar shops where I choose 3 of this item, 4 of that, and so on until I run out of steam. I am not a happy shopper. I struggle with feelings of excess as I lug loads of bags around and inevitably I end up with not bringing enough back. I feel embarrassed in the presence of my family who surely must think I am loaded and rubbing it in their face every time I am home. It is far from the truth. I am simply spending my annual clothes and shoes budget in one week. I would much rather be

---

[5] White goods are essential kitchen electrical appliances, e.g. fridge freezer, washing machine, etc. It is important to note that in some cultures dryers are not considered essential white goods; neither are ovens. Microwave ovens are readily available and a landlord will usually supply one on request.

able to wander to the shops when I trash a favourite top or shirt and spend a pleasurable hour or two mixing and matching, not to mention looking for a bargain. Of course, all this becomes much more problematic when I am living in summertime and vacationing in winter.

b.   What OTC medicines should you bring with you? If you have a product that works well for you, bring enough to last you while you are in your new post initially. You may not be able to get the same brand from a pharmacy or on prescription, so be prepared.

c.   If you are under medical care for an existing condition that requires the consumption of regular meds, again, take enough prescription medicine with you until you are confident you can seamlessly continue treatment with the same product.

d.   Do you have a penchant for certain shampoos, creams, toothpastes, sanitary items? Again, bring enough until you can source replacements, particularly sanitary items for your size and flow.

e.   Should you bring work resources? Absolutely! If you have a right to use resources you have created or permission to use co-created resources, put them in your bag. You may be moving to a similar economic zone but the language is different so while the resources may be available, and maybe even better resources, they may not be accessible to you initially. Conversely, you may be moving to a lesser economic zone where your resources will inject exciting new life-blood.

f.   Should you bring food? Yes, no, and depends. Yes, if you are coeliac or gluten intolerant. Bring some rice cakes to keep you going initially. Or if you are diabetic; bring some Stevia. No, if you have no special dietary requirements. Go with the flow but stay away from street corner vendors for the first few weeks until your gut adjusts to the different bacteria found locally and you get advice on where is safe to eat. Depends - if you have an existing comfort habit around a particular product, bring enough while you experiment with what is available locally. Depends where you are travelling to also. Do your research. If you have special needs, be prepared. Jet lag can be debilitating. If you have supplies for a few days, it is one less thing to worry about.

3. Most people opt for a partial move. It allows them some comfort at a reduced cost. It leaves the way open to insert some local furniture, art work, or other materials into the living space. Carefully chosen, it also provides the comfort items from home that children, and adults, like to surround themselves with.

I always include the following in a small shipment:

a. Towels. I love a decent size towel with some soft soakage. They are not always readily available. Neither are tea towels if you are a 'drying the dishes' person.

b. Bedding. In our move to Prague I came to love the big pillows they use there. I bring 2 big pillows and a few sets of pillow cases as these are not widely available. The guest room has local pillows. Some are really interesting but I have not found a replacement I prefer yet.

c. I bring a big duvet and covers if I have space, especially if we are moving to a cold area.

d. Books. I put in as many in my shipment as I can fit, both those I have had for a while and new ones I can look forward to read. My Kindle, I carry in my bag.

e.   Cutlery. I love a decent knife and fork, and I have several sets of nice chop sticks from my time in Japan.

f.   Crockery. We have a set of plates and mugs which we have hauled around the world, every one still in great condition. They are for eating the way we like to eat while leaving room to add local designs if we find something we really like.

The shipment consideration is a small but crucial part of the big picture. Two months into your posting you will be very happy you have included something familiar. Now, what will you do with:

- Your house or apartment if you own one? Will you sell it, rent it or leave it vacant? Think ahead. If you plan to return home annually, where will you stay? Whether you are single or a family unit, comfort and costs need consideration. What do you need in a return visit?

    o   Personal space. This may be a strange consideration to put first since you have been on your own all year. Returning can bring smothering challenges of the best kind and intense 24/7 connection time that leaves you exhausted and grumpy. Jet lag may be a factor you have to cope with simultaneously. You have changed yet your past 'home' environment and people seem not to have.

    o   A place to stay

    o   A way to travel

    o   Money - lots of it. Many expats speak of feeling hard-done-by when they spend their hard-earned savings to visit family and relatives only to experience arguments and disharmony. More on this later.

Why am I mentioning this here when you have not even left yet? Because the first instinct is to make a clean break, wipe the slate behind you, burn all your bridges. This may well be the best option for you but think ahead for a bit before you commit to such final action. You may consider property left behind you as:

- o A rope around your neck dragging you back
- o An anchor or a possible port in a storm
- o An investment for the future

In one family of 4 that I discussed this with, all three views were presented without any prompting. The father felt it was a rope around his neck, the mother and son needed the anchor, and that daughter thought it was a wonderful investment for the future.

- Goods you are not bringing with you? Will you sell them in a garage sale, online, by local advertising? Beware, these may take some time to shift, and it can be a very emotional journey, this taking apart of your life. It can also be very freeing, very affirming, a true 'out with the old, in with the new' experience. Will you store them until your return? Many expats I have spoken to tell the 'giving-away' story, and it is one I can personally relate to. I have given away so many goods in each of my moves. Sometimes I cannot find a suitable replacement in my new home or I pay through the nose for it. Once the decision to leave is made, it is easier to part with items somehow.

- How will you deal with acquisitive family and friends? Because you are leaving the country, there seems to be some unexplained tacit agreement that you will be up for a good deal, maybe even a free one! If you give a friend or family member an item to use while you are away, you should consider it gone. White goods will wear out. Cars will break down. The piano becomes so much a part of someone else's life it seems churlish to repossess. And if they give you back your old, now-battered, one and buy the state of the art replacement for themselves, what hit will your friendship take? Because – here is another unsaid and unproven assumption – anyone who goes abroad to work must be loaded! You must be making a packet!

For now, every decision you make is laden with outcomes that become increasingly difficult to manage seamlessly as you pull away. Become adept at thinking forward from where you are, and back from where you will be, around every decision. Be proactive. Be decisive. Tie up the stuff you are leaving behind properly. Make it clear whether you want it used, stored or disposed of. Sign off on the shipment. Get those necessary vaccinations. Close your bag. You are as ready as you can be.

Some thoughts to consider from Barbara on her personal journey and approach as you leave:

Although I remained in Europe for my first expat experience as a native English speaker I had to deal with another language. I had school French and German which helped a bit with learning Czech. Even the Irish helped, believe it or not.

First things first - learn the numbers for money etc. Listen to announcements and locals speaking. Absorb the language before you really start on lessons. Ask your local co-workers for advice. Lonely Planet is pretty good on what to do and what not to do in countries. For goodness sake know some of the history of the country you move to!!! Good idea to know current president and prime minister and which party is in power. Always a good idea in your own country too!!!! Local people will want to learn from you about back home.

Obey the rules – even if you don't like them or they are different from what you know. Be patient with bureaucracy and with officials, just as you would in your own country, I hope!

Remember even if your job requires you to live and work in this new country you are essentially a guest. How do you expect foreigners to act back where you come from?

I have also lived way out of the European culture zone. Believe me if you are in Asia it is very different. You do need to know local customs, some key phrases and really listen when you are being orientated and again find out about the place before you go. If the country is a strongly faith orientated place you really do need to be careful and especially if you are female. It is important! Remember the adage .... when in Rome ...

Learn to enjoy living in another country which is different from your own in some ways or many ways. You can have an amazing time and really develop personally. You can have fun! I know. I have!

4

JOURNEY OUT

THERE IS NOTHING more traumatic than leaving your tearful mother who is living with cancer or crippled in a wheelchair. We have done both. Are we proud about it? It is the wrong question to ask but since it is asked, we would both say,' No! Absolutely not!' The simple truth for us was that we could not make a living in our home-country. We left because we were going nowhere fast and we wanted a different future for us and our children. We weren't going far initially but it may as well have been the other side of the moon! In point of fact, we weren't at home anyway; we were half way across the country, a phone call away. But we were on the same piece of ground and that in the end is what mattered. Living on another island was perceived as further away than it was in reality. We were moving from Dublin to London.

While both women celebrated our success, as we did, it came as an emotional sacrifice for all parties. Now, that's way beyond a choice. That's a choice with a bite in the ass, literally. In the midst of the excitement and the validation, it was really hard to go.

It is entirely natural to feel 'alone' and 'lonely' as you leave. If this is the first time you have gone abroad, you may be feeling truly alone for the first time in your life. 'Alone' and 'loneliness' are different yet the context in which they present is often very similar, so similar in fact, that one is often thought of as the other although this is not so. 'Alone' is an acute sense of self: it is inward focussed. You are suddenly and overwhelmingly identified with 'you' as a singular entity, apart from all around you. It is a slightly detached state of mind which lingers for a short time. It almost comes as a surprise to be 'alone'. You can be 'alone' by yourself or in the middle of party; sitting on the beach or being hustled on a crowded street; waiting in a queue or shoving through Black Friday sales[6]. 'Loneliness', by comparison, is a deep feeling focussed on the absence of another; it is other focus, unlike the state of being 'alone', which is intensely present for only a short time. Loneliness lingers. It twirls its tendrils around your heart, and if you are not aware of this, it can choke all your joy away. Keep your reason, or reasons, for leaving clear in your mind, and move forward. Loneliness only thrives when you pay it attention. Shift your attention and the feelings fade. And as you move away you will have lots of new and exciting things to focus on!

WAYS OF LEAVING There are a number of different ways you can physically leave. Certain factors will play a part on your decision. These are:

- Events surrounding your leaving: If you are fleeing for your life you will welcome any option to escape. If your leaving is a well-considered choice, your behaviour will be different.
- Culture: Historical factors in your current culture will present defined options you may feel obliged to comply with. For

---

[6] Black Friday sales are held on the Friday after Thanksgiving in the US. They get their name from the throng of people who hustle outside department stores to get that discounted present for a loved one, including oneself, for Christmas.

example, there is a history of 'waking'[7] the traveller in Ireland based upon the memories from the famine years in the 1840s when immigrants would leave without an option of returning or even the promise of a safe passage across the Atlantic. In essence, the person leaving would have a ritualistic funeral gathering and meal. The memories from these occasions lie deep in the genes of the Irish still despite the proliferation of safe travelling options and the evidence of citizens returning to visit regularly.

- How far you are travelling: If you are moving to the next country or state there may be no fuss at all! In this modern world, there are many budget airlines that means 'home' is only an hour or two away.

- Leaving by yourself: This engenders more protectiveness than if you were leaving as part of a group, particularly if you are a young female. Whatever your gender, it is likely that you will have to argue your case positively several times and be prepared for dire warnings. It costs nothing to listen politely. Who knows – their words may indeed keep you out of trouble.

- Leaving with a family: You will have a lot more preparation to do in this case. The emotion around a family move is different. You are leaving with a ready-made support group and the leaving is deemed easier, which it is. However, expect more emotion around young children. You will have to manage comments carefully and support your children with positive reinforcement around your family move.

So, how to do it? You can:

---

[7] An Irish 'wake' traditionally comprises 2 parts. On the night the person dies they are not left alone. Family and neighbours sit with the corpse all night remembering his or her life and praying for the repose of his or her soul until the body is taken to the church the next day or evening. The following day, after the deceased is buried, the family invites mourners to join them for a meal. This joining together for a meal is what is reminiscent in 'waking' the traveller.

- Leave quietly; slip away undetected under the radar to avoid complications.
- Have a going-away party with your friends. Question here – should you include your family in this? It depends on a variety of things but the most likely answer is 'no'. Consider:
  - Are you on speaking terms with your family?
  - Do they live near you or you them?
  - Are you still living at home?
  - Do they get on with your friends?
- Have a going-away party or dinner with your family. Will you include your friends here? This answer is simple. I suggest you only include a significant-other here unless your friends are part of your whole family community. Even then, I would suggest you decide in favour of your family. You can always meet your mates separately. Consider too, who is paying? It is to be expected that 'he who pays the piper, calls the tune!'
- Then there is the work-leaving occasion. It is a sign of character to be present for this regardless of the hows and whys of your leaving. Accept words of commendation, and any gifts, with equanimity. If it is a formal occasion, prepare a few short sentences in response. Remember why you went to work there in the first place. This is a time for political correctness not personality conflicts. Remember too, you may well be asking the boss for a reference in the future.

One thing I do advise is that you make the time to see all the people who have supported your life journey so far. You never know when you will get to see them again. There is no need to turn this into a series of big occasions. A handshake or hug, and a thank you, will suffice.

As you pick up your luggage to go you can be assailed by a number of emotions, including the fear, anxiety and excitement you encountered in your decision making process. These are never far away in your life journey anyway and they do select sensitive times to catch our attention. This is one of them, a moment of huge vulnerability. Shift your attention to your reason or reasons for leaving and excitement will lead; pay attention to your personal insecurities and fear or anxiety will lead. You have a singular moment of choice. Vote for your decision and move on. Expect feelings of lightness and freedom with excitement; heaviness and doom with fear and anxiety.

It is also likely that you will experience the following:

- Fatigue or a feeling of being drained– it is likely that you have not got enough rest in the last few weeks. Excitement alone will keep you restless at night not to mention any farewell partying. Fear and anxiety will drain you emotionally and physically.

- Headaches – from dehydration and emotional stress. Make sure you drink enough WATER.

- Weight loss or weight gain or bloating. Prolonged anxiety states will interfere with your digestion, as will lack of sleep, or an interrupted routine, or extended routine as you hurry to get everything in order. Prolonged excitement will push your metabolism into overdrive; people may begin to wonder what you are on! Space yourself and remember to eat properly. You are burning up more body fuel than usual; make sure you replenish your cells with healthy eating and plenty of water.

- If you are flying for the first time inform yourself as much as possible about procedures and time keeping. Be prepared. There is nothing to be anxious about. Airline staff and ground staff are there to help, make your journey as comfortable as possible, and to keep you safe.

It always amazes me that the pinnacle of personal achievement, when one should be on an emotional high, is often laced with intense separation pain. It is as if you need the one in juxtaposition to the other to appreciate it fully. I do feel that we create elastic attachment cords to those whom we care about; leaving does not diminish the caring but it does stretch the cord, often to breaking point. Sometimes 'breaking' the cord is what is necessary. The person leaving holds the responsibility along with the choice; you are the one who leaves, who pulls away. The strength in the cord, the strength of the attachment, will determine how often you bounce back. You may, of course, draw people to you but do not depend on it. If it happens, and it does, treat it as a joyful opportunity to show them into your new world so they may be enhanced by it too. If you are pulled back, expect to face the same irritations that encouraged you to leave in the first place. They will not have gone away; in fact, it is likely you will experience these even more intensely since you will now know what it is like to live without them!

But not everyone experiences separation pain. If you go with support and encouragement like Sara did, that anticipation and the excitement may well lead to a story like hers. She writes of her first time abroad:

"The first leap outside of ourselves. Beyond all concepts of normal. Into the complete unknown. No wonder it stays with us forever.

My first move abroad was by far my favourite. Whether it was the anticipation, the venture into 'the rest of the world', the novelty or the gorgeous country of Chile itself, I can never be sure. Either way, my short six months living with a Chilean family and studying Spanish at a prestigious, local University, transformed my passion for language into the wanderlust that propels my life today. It eliminated any fears I might have had about living abroad. After my first move, accepting a summer job in Italy, finishing my fourth year teaching in Shanghai and planning the next move to Bangkok has become my new normal.

The beauty of the first move was probably its nuance. Everything was new and therefore, amazing. A simple meal of beef and rice was made magical by exotic new spices and hot sauce. I feel in love with Nescafe and anything smothered in avocado or that sweet, Chilean caramel called manjar. I took notes on every detail and noticed even the smallest differences between my previous existence in Minnesota and my new life in Viña del Mar, Chile. A simple walk to school was full of adventure. I noticed the subtle curves in the hilly road, the immense sky over the ocean, the fanning bird of paradise plants, the secure gates surrounding each house, the way small dogs inside the gates intimidated me as I passed, the obnoxious cat calls from the construction workers ten stories up and an intense feeling of pride as I walked into my University. Although it has been seven years since I was in Chile and the journal I had so carefully kept ended up being stolen, I still remember every image, scent and sensation. It is truly as though they have made an 'imprint' on me. Since leaving Chile it seems to have never left me. All my future travels and adventures are connected with and compared to my first, most influential 'imprint move'.

No matter where I am in the world I seem to see Chile. I see the hilly Pacific Ocean at beaches in Taiwan, the grand Andes in the French Alps, the arid sands and ancient ruins of the Atacama in Western China, the cacti and wind-shaped landscapes of Santiago's outskirts in Sardinia and the lush vegetation of Chile's South in Thailand's tropics. No matter how many more beaches, mountains, deserts, landscapes or varieties of vegetation I come to in my lifetime, none will be experienced with the same level of intensity as those in Chile."

First moves hold a magical quality for most expats. The newness draws one in; the anticipation can be almost unbelievable. Everything about that first new culture move will be challenging and fresh; it is up to you to make it one of the best times of your life, or not. How you perceive your new world will depend on whether you are a glass half-full person, glass half-empty person or a realist. An optimist is perceived as a glass half-full person; a pessimist as a glass half-empty person; and a realist as the one who says the glass is bigger than it need be anyway!

Whatever your personality this new move will change the way you see the world from now on. In this first journey you will compare everything you find against your previous home experience. You will look for the same products you used; the same programmes on TV. And you will learn new ways of living, and these new lessons will change your expectations for the future. Living abroad will imprint your life with either a positive or negative image of what living away from home actually feels like. The imprint of your first new culture experience is so strong I call this first expat move **The Imprint Move**. All future moves are more likely to be measured against this Imprint Move rather than your home culture life experiences.

The Imprint Move

Every location move we make brings with it new challenges and possibilities but none brings more potent change than the Imprint Move. I define this as our first foreign-language move. This is the one that leaves us in one exhilarating and painful moment on the very top of our game and utterly disempowered simultaneously. We have consciously left our comfort zone for the stretch zone. We get off the plane at the peak of our challenge-performance and enter a world where even the simplest of communication is challenging.

The Imprint Move changes us deeply. It causes us learn adaptive skills like we did as two-year olds. We are frustrated by knowing what we want but incapable of communicating at the level we have developed in order to be here in the first place. We are like a young child learning to communicate orally for the first time. We point to objects we want; we become expert at miming.(Pointing and miming can become embedded in the subconscious; I still find myself pointing to a menu and miming even when I go home until the strange looks I invariably get penetrate my brain, and blushing, I finally give up until the next time!) Like children developing their language skills, we learn the new vocabulary of our immediate surroundings first, and then we gradually expand to short sentences and, depending on our language-learning abilities, go on to learn more complex sentence structure. We reach a sufficient proficiency for where we are and we plateau to consolidate our learning, just like as a child. We remain at this language level or we may continue later. Time will inform us.

But it is not all about language. Language is only a part of culture. Research today suggests that language defines a culture: a more complex language reveals a more sophisticated and expressive culture. To survive, as well as to thrive, in a foreign culture, expats need to be adaptive. We need to understand the norms, the context of the norms; and decide which we need to embrace to succeed. Clashes occur when we come up against cultural norms that contrast negatively with our values: the culture clash is born. This calls for graciousness on our part; we are the foreigner. We are here to experience how others live not to bend them to our will. We are explorers not conquerors. But the more we 'live the world' the less gracious we are likely to be. We 'adhere' to cultures we favour to a point where the line blurs in our subconscious: we are foreign yet have lived this culture long enough to have a voice. We begin to see it as home perhaps. For the majority of us, this is unreal. We are foreigners. A select few can fully bridge the culture gaps. Foreigners embrace them as one of their own. These select few not only have a voice; they have a disproportionately influential voice.

But all the while we are learning about this new culture and being changed by it, the local people who work with us are learning about our culture from us. They change irrevocably too. We are Ambassadors for our homeland whether or not we have lived there all our lives up to now or have lived in several other countries before turning up here. We are defined by our nationality globally. We are what our passports say we are. We may not think we are but others will. This may cause us some internal stress but no matter how much we explain about our multi-journeys to this point, we carry our national identity squarely for all to see. It is an interesting dilemma; we may believe we have moved away significantly from our national identity as we have moved towards our new cultures. We may no more resemble our 'national' self when we first left home than a random expat on the street of our new culture but it still defines us. We need to remain respectful to our nationality.

Expanding further on the Imprint Move, it is the Move where we:

- Are affirmed in our ability to live outside our Formative Culture. We survive, and then thrive.
- Benefit financially from the experience; or benefit deeply in another way that is in accordance with out talents and values.
- Give more than we would be able to in our home culture or have the opportunity to. As Winston Churchill said: 'We make a living by what we get but we make a life by what we give'.
- Expand our world vision from a completely different perspective. We begin to see the world through new culture filters.
- Learn adaptive communication skills. We begin to recognise the universality of humankind through this experience. Gestures of pointing and miming are how children communicate the world over; suddenly we have something in common to begin with. The human condition is universal. People have the same physical needs wherever they live in the world. Parents want the best for their children. Our base emotions and reflexes are mirrored worldwide. A frightened

person is recognisable the world over. Surprisingly, not so much a happy person.

- Imprint our brains with a new cultural identity. We literally become a different person.
- Understand the process of negotiation through personal experience. Our core values may be challenged in this process. Expats often move on when core values are challenged.

5

THE 24 HOUR CROSSOVER

THE THING ABOUT 'leaving' is that it is not just about you. The thing about 'arriving' is that it is all about you. It is a singular moment of complete selfishness on your journey to maximising your potential. And guess what? It's addictive!

You've arrived! Congratulations! By the end of the next 24 hours you will be considerably integrated into your new life. Faces will be put to the voices behind the emails and the telephone calls; yours for them, theirs for you. Both sides size each other up simultaneously. It is, at worst, an intense evaluation moment; at best, a fantastic validation that you have done the right thing; you are in the right place. It can be a struggle to be at your best after the journey but it is important you give it a good shot. If you have arrived directly from a long haul flight you may well wish you had the opportunity for a shower and a change of clothes first. Don't worry. The vast majority of

> The first 24 hours is all about you. It is full of 'Aha' moments; moments of confirmation that you are in the right place.

people travelling inwards for work will be in exactly the same boat. Freshen up. Smile broadly. And walk into your future. The magic has begun!

"My husband and I had always wanted to travel and when our children were both in University the opportunity came for us to live and work in Tokyo. We flew into Tokyo in mid-August when the humidity is at its highest. We had heard tales of this but nothing quite prepared us for the sensory impact of that first step into sauna-like conditions!

By the end of our 12 hour overnight flight we were stiff and sore; we were travelling in Economy but were well looked after. We had celebrated with a gin and tonic after take-off and enjoyed wine with our main meal; after all we were celebrating a new chapter in our lives and deserved the relaxed downtime we were experiencing. We slept fitfully, and in hindsight didn't take near enough water, so on arrival we rather groggily and stiffly made our way through the incredibly ordered process of disembarkation that typifies Narita Airport. In a startlingly short time we were standing in the Baggage Hall, eyes on stalks, waiting for our bags, a new stamp in our passports. The atmosphere was calm; the aircon whispered around us, shielding us from the reality that awaited us outside.

Bags in cart, we made our way towards the Exit to be met by the boss and his driver, Sugito san, who had parked the bus as close to the doors as possible and even rolled out the red carpet. His small bit of English exceeded our tiny bit of Japanese but he didn't seem to mind; he was pleased with our paltry, faltering Arigato Gozimasu. We were completely unprepared for the assault on our senses that followed; which, in fact, stayed with us for the next few weeks and months.

The door opened and we stepped out into a sauna. The heat and humidity literally took our breath away. We perspired on the spot without moving a muscle. We were transfixed. Sugito san rushed ahead and opened the doors for us and we clambered into the welcoming coolness of the airconed interior. We could feel sweat dripping down our backs soaking our trouser bands, and even trickling further down than we were prepared for! Sweat dripped unhindered down our faces. It was horrible! The diminutive Sugito san hauled our suitcases effortlessly into the bus and we were off. He was well prepared; he even had soothing Japanese music for us to relax to.

The 90 minute journey enthralled us even as we fought to stay awake. The first part was through lovely countryside and we soaked up the differences we were seeing through our windows. The city appeared in the distance and before long we were immersed in the huge city that is Tokyo. What a wonderful sight! We travelled under bridges, over bridges, parallel to bridges, often hundreds of metres in the air, through high rise and low rise until we arrived at our destination, a modern five story school in the heart of Shibuya Ward. We were burned out with excitement; we were exhausted. But there were formalities to be undertaken. We signed forms, drank water, toured the facility, made suitable accommodating appraisals, and then we were back in the bus to be taken to our home for the next 4 years. Imai san had put in some basic provisions for us, including the required earthquake kit which she proceeded to explain to us in detail. In truth, we took in little of what she said right then; we had reached total immersion point. Finally, several hours after we touched down, we were alone, that is, apart from the hundreds of cicadas that were serenading us from the trees outside. We had arrived."

The first 24 hours is all about you. It is full of 'Aha' moments; moments of confirmation that you are in the right place. After all, you are here by choice. That choice speaks to the moment in hand, and the rest of your life.

There are 4 moments in particular I suggest you watch out for and acknowledge.

- The 'I did it!' moment. This is a quiet, internal moment of intense excitement. It can present as you move through the disembarkation process or when the door closes and you are alone for the first time in your new house, apartment or hotel room, or anywhere in between. It is like you are giving yourself a secret hug. It is a lovely moment of self-growth. It is the well of deep strength that will see you through the next weeks and months.

- The "in situ' moment. This is a 'wonder' moment. You have arrived and your senses are working overtime ogling your new environment. Your feet are on the ground and it feels good. Your self-talk will run the script 'I am actually here' ad infinitum. You are self-confirming the truth of your presence in this foreign place.

- The 'total immersion' moment. You will recognise this moment when you get there. You will simply stop taking things in. Your brain has taken on all the newness it can reasonably cope with and drives you to seek solitude and physical renewal. You are seeing all that is going on, and hearing every word said, but your processing faculties have retreated to deal with all that has gone before first. You are essentially in a waking trance.

- The 'what have I done' moment. Behind the excitement, and the validation, and the self-growth, your habitual self is out of synch with where you now find yourself so it should come as no great surprise that your past self will look for its usual patterns of life and living that are no more, and will challenge your thinking on the way things now are. The strengths of these thoughts grow in proportion to your fatigue, and you are going to feel fatigued, stretched in all ways, in the next few weeks in particular. Recognise them in the over-the-top emotional responses that are just not you. For example, you cannot initially regulate the shower temperature as easily as in your old place so you get angry at it. You hear yourself say 'this bloody thing doesn't work properly!' Before long, everything doesn't work properly! Properly according to what? Your past life! You have encountered the up close and personal cliff-edge of adjustment. First thing in the morning, this can set the tone for the day unless you grab it in time. In an Expat move in a very different culture, everything is a learning curve. Cut yourself some slack. Give yourself some extra time and – remember why you are here.

Welcome to the new you. Whatever the future holds, you can always look back on this 24 hours and know, without a shadow of a doubt, that you can do more than you think you can, always. How amazing is that! You have started to live your dream. You can now move forward to work, live and be the person you always wanted to be. In short, you can now remake yourself. There is no one here to say, 'Isn't that Johnny's young lad?' or 'Isn't that Mary's young girl?' You have a clean slate. You will be taken at face value.

When you meet people for the first time at your new destination they see you as you are. They are expecting an expat, a professional, a brave person who has travelled a serious distance, braved language barriers, and that is who they see. Do you recognise yourself here? They take in your demeanour; how you are dressed; how you present yourself. They are prepared to take you as they see you. How freeing is that! You have talked the talk to get here; now you can walk the walk! In fact, not to do so can lead to confusion. You are truly free to be the person you want to be. The ball is firmly in your court.

One short or long journey has opened the door to a new life for you. Congratulate yourself on getting this far. But be aware too that while your expectations have undeniably changed it is too soon to expect deep and lasting change on the inside. You will have taken your personal baggage with you, the negative as well as the positive. For example, if you experienced low self-esteem at home, it is still with you, and it will raise its head in this new location until you are affirmed otherwise. For now, you have plucked yourself out of one geographical situation and dropped yourself in a new one. You are still essentially the same on the inside. The next few weeks, months and years, even a lifetime, will give you the opportunity to nurture and build the character you desire on the inside. Go live your dream!

In the first few weeks in particular pay close attention to the language you use around situations, in particular:

Listen to yourself saying:
- I like . . .
- I wish . . .
- I wonder . . . statements.

Banish immediately the sentences that start with:
- I can't . . .
- I shouldn't . . .
- I couldn't . . . statements.

The former set of statements will empower you while the latter will hold you back, will drag you down, and restrict your success. Our brain hears what we say and will work to provide us with the experience we articulate. You are here to succeed, right? Start as you mean to go on.

CHOOSE WHERE YOU LIVE WITH CARE
Many staff feel they must accept the accommodation their company provides for them without question, and this may well be non-negotiable but beneficial and necessary for a variety of reasons.

Their company may be over-mindful that the quality of the accommodation and its location reflects the prestigious position of the incoming person to the work community. All is wonderful if there is a happy congruence of location and living factors. Where, and how, they choose to house you or advise you on housing reflects their thinking around your status or its direct opposite. Pay close attention to this. Be aware that the person sourcing your home may never have lived outside their home country so will approach your expat expectations from a local comparison measuring stick. If you know what suits you from a location and living situation from the beginning, your new HR Dept. will be happy to accommodate you appropriately but they are not mind-readers. You need to discuss your needs with them. Many HR Depts. work on the basis that foreigners expect a certain calibre of accommodation and may find it confusing if you are requesting a more ordinary solution in less salubrious surroundings.

If you are unsure or uncertain in your way forward, take the accommodation. See how it works out. You may get to love living in a new way. If not, do start a dialogue with your company. It may take some time to work out a replacement for a variety of local logistical reasons.

Choose your living accommodation for the way you want to live. Most expats either want to live near where they work to lessen the commute time or they want to live well away from work to have more of a private life. Consider also the implications for accompanying spouse or family, particularly if someone accompanying you will be at home most of the time.

These two scenarios are explored in the following statements and questions:

Statement: I want to live near where I work to minimise travel.

Consider the following questions carefully:

Q: How do you want to live outside work?

Q: Is it good to be surrounded by co-workers outside work too?

Q: Are there amenities nearby that I want to use?

Q: Will I be spending all my non-working time travelling for social amenities? How much will that cost? What are my available travel options from here?

Q: What about family members? How will this living situation suit them?

Q: How do I rate the convenience of a quiet place to grab a drink or a coffee?

Q: Do I want to live next door to a night club?

Q: Is it wise to live next door to a red light district?

Q: What noise levels will I experience from airplanes, highways, adjacent Emergency Hospitals, traffic congestion in general?

Statement: I want to live well away from where I work.

Q: How far is enough?

Q: How long will it take me to travel to work? How will I get there? How much will it cost?

Q: What amenities are available in my 'home' location?

Q: What will I do at the weekend?

Q: How will this location suit my accompanying partner, family?

Q: How will they get to work, school, social events?

Q: Will this location be too isolated, too lonely?

Some people will not have a choice where they live when they move abroad to work and live. Their employer may house them for convenience sake or safety reasons and this is non-negotiable. In this event, you are likely to be housed with other expat staff either from your own workplace or another. This can happen at all stages of workforce, management, and leadership. There may be financial advantages available as a consequence and the arrangement may make perfect sense in the given environment. However, it is always restrictive whether you are in a top suite of a luxury hotel or in a dormitory with bunk beds in a row. And you are unlikely to experience a truly integrative new culture way of living. You may however experience many different other cultures within your living situation. There is good in all of it, and challenges too. Just be prepared. Know yourself, and how you are likely to respond should you find your freedoms curtailed.

6

NEW BEGINNINGS

DO YOU REMEMBER when you learned to ride a bicycle? Or drive a car? Do you remember the excitement, the nervousness, the mistakes as you bit by bit put all the actions together in the correct order to make it all work smoothly, safely and correctly? It took a few tries, right, before you could read while riding a bicycle or talk to a passenger while driving a car? Well, your new move to this new culture will be like that. It will take a while until you are up and running smoothly and comfortably. What defines your experiences is not what or whom you come across but how you respond to these new stimuli.

It is easy to experience sensory overload at a time like this; the more exotic the location the more it is to be expected. What exhilarates one person stupefies another so it is easy to give, and make, an initial false impression to your new local circle and other new expats. Travel fatigue and personal circumstances are played down; Expat is the one label in town and there are expectations and requirements on you from the start. But this is what you have planned for, waited for. Sometimes the rush is too much; sometimes its absence is worrying. Your professionalism got you through the first 24 hours without embarrassing yourself. Now can you keep that going as you are bombarded by a myriad of new experiences in the coming weeks? The first six weeks are incredibly full-on with everything so new; these are challenging for everyone on the job, building a life in a new culture.

I remember clearly how insane those first few weeks in Tokyo were. It was my first foreign language posting and I didn't know the language. I was confident that I would learn enough to get by in time but I hadn't reckoned with the vast majority of road signs being in Japanese only. Well, why not? It is Japan. Why would they have all signage in English? I didn't know then that many Japanese people do speak English and that I could get help with directions from the majority of stores anyway. So in my expat isolated world I travelled tentatively keeping close to home. The fear of getting lost, of not being able to tell anyone where I was, was very real.

The Tokyo train system is extensive and excellent value for money but since the entire population of Ireland passed through Shinjuku station alone every single day near where I lived, I was stupefied by its vastness. The transfer tunnels criss-crossed with frightening frequency; it reminded me of underground rivers, the constant motion of the people being the rippling waters, that is, until the desired platform was reached. Then the river became a lake of people all intending to get on the train at the station even if they had to be pushed on by designated pushers. After experiencing this phenomenon on a few occasions I made a decision to avoid such peak travel times. I am taller than most Japanese, including men, and in those squash situations I would invariably end up with some male head resting against my boobs to his delight and my chagrin! Another station, Shibuya, had the busiest crossing in the world outside its doors. I would stand on one side of the road intending to cross diagonally and would be dismayed at the sea of black-clad individuals I could see massing on the other side! How on earth could I get across without being hassled and bumped out of my trajectory and as a consequence, fearfully lose my direction? And while I waited, an equally immense build-up of people was happening on my side of the road behind me. It was truly staggering to pass directly across these junctions. The Japanese are unfailingly polite and have set patterns of traversing that make such feats calm and steady; I only had to go with the flow. And that's how I managed in those first few weeks: I went with the flow, increasing my circle of ability bit by bit until it became second-nature to me to walk around Tokyo without any fear whatsoever.

THE LEARNING CURVE in the next 6 weeks is immense. You have to learn new ways of:

- Communicating
- Working
- Travelling
- Eating
- Sleeping
- Dressing
- Crossing the road
- Reading the signs
- Remembering directions
- Remembering foreign names
- Remembering and using protocols
- Cooking
- Washing
- Shopping
- Calling home
- Getting a haircut
- Managing medical appointments

- Dealing with different time zones
- Coping with a new climate
- And lots, lots more

You will meet new:
- Friends
- Managers
- Customers
- Trainers
- Competent people
- Incompetent people
- Meddlers
- Inscrutables
- Bullies
- In short, the whole gamut of people you were familiar with in a previous lifetime but who sing to a different cultural tune.

You will experience:
- New roles
- Changes to your usual role
- Same role but new context – and context does matter a whole lot.

But it is often in your personal life you find the most challenge. Your work life is structured from the word go, and often in your home language. It offers an anchor, a sense of familiarity that makes a difference. But once you leave work you find yourself alone. There is no one to hand who can help with adjusting the aircon; no one to translate when you need three slices of cheese at the supermarket. You live each day thriving and surviving; sometimes you just want to curl up with some comfort food and remember what it was like to be in control!

Comfort food serves a variety of purposes. It defines your Formative Culture[8]. For people who have made several moves in a lifetime, whether voluntarily or part of family life choices, they reach a stage where they are unsure where their Formative Culture is. This can be identified in those comfort food moments because you often reach for your favourite foods you used when you felt 'at home'. The same pattern is identified in people frequenting a favourite restaurant or pub; the location is familiar, safe and comforting. People are, for the most part, ritualistic creatures of habit. Reaching for comfort food defines your stress levels. Doing so is often an indication that you are experiencing overload; that you have moved past your stretch zone into your panic zone. This holds true in all of life's experiences; when you reach for comfort food, recognise you are feeling overloaded. But the amazing thing is, comfort food settles your stress level; consuming the tastes of 'home' re-establishes the feeling of calm. Incredibly, you may not even like the food anymore but it still impacts your subconscious, rolling out those feel-good memory links that really work! Comfort food used on occasions like these is very useful: used continuously, it alerts you to deeper feelings of unhappiness, lack of meaning, and/or balance in your life. Beware – comfort food eating born of loneliness and overload can also become a destructive habit that will last. Smoking and alcohol feature as comfort food too.

> But there are too many 'quiet' expats living dead lives in the dreamland they choose as home.

For trailing spouses or partners with no accompanying children, an international move can be extremely difficult for they have no work-identity from the start. It is really important for them to find a way forward quickly; to make new friends; have a reason for getting out of bed in the morning. Many will find some work with the host business

---

[8] Formative Culture is the home culture of where you grew up, particularly those early years when home memories are deeply rooted.

their partner works for; even if part time and not within their field of expertise, this can be a lifeline. For those who make friends easily they can have a blast and not want to work at all! But there are too many 'quiet' expats living dead lives in the dreamland they choose as home. These are resourceful, private, intelligent people and they will work out a way forward in time hopefully. In a strange paradox, this time may be the turning point of their lives as they have time to think and review their values; study for new opportunities; and create entirely new lives for themselves. But to say that having all this free time on their hands in an exotic location is 'really living the life' is a misnomer. The strain on relationships can be devastating.

Ildiko writes:

My biggest challenge as an expat is the language. If you don't speak the language, you're isolated from the beginning. But even if you don't, start to work anywhere, at anything, because this is how you hear it and begin to pick it up. And don't even feel bad if you get it wrong when you begin to speak because this is how you learn. Ignore the mean 'What!" from unhelpful locals and other expats as you struggle to get the pronunciation correct. I ask, would you like to speak with me in Hungarian then?

Culture in another country is different. Expect high days and low days. When people say 'I don't miss my country' I feel very sad for them. I don't understand that. If you have a family, it is easier for your child to settle in because of school because that is in a language he or she will be able to understand. The same for the spouse who is working; their same-language environment makes it easier to settle in. But for the spouse who doesn't have a job to go to, the local environment is always foreign, every single day!

Living as an expat I see a lot of different lifestyles. I have the choice to stay if I like it; move away if I don't. Living this way I can see and experience the world. Travelling is good thing. Meeting people and experiencing other cultures has broadened my mind and expanded my expectations from life. Living this way has opened the world to us as a family. It is our decision to make the most of it or not.

In my recent move to Shanghai, the one thing I would change right away is my old apartment. We took it too quickly. My advice to anyone else is to take time to find the right place. Know what is important to you and keep looking. It is easy to take something really quickly because you're tired and just want to get settled in. I would like people to know too that the cost of living can be expensive as an expat. The minute they see an expat the price goes up, and I mean really up! If you can get a Chinese friend to help with big items that will save you a lot of money. It can be hard to find a job too unless you're a teacher, an engineer or a doctor. In China, you need to be able to speak the local language for most jobs. But if you get the chance, however small, take it. Don't be afraid. You'll never know where it will lead to. And you'll have some money of your own again.

I am amazed at what parents do to their children. The after-school clubs and extra tuition; putting them into foreign language schools where they don't understand a word and expecting them to be top of the class; sending them boarding half-way around the world; leaving the ayi to raise them, to name a few. Parents seem too busy here to spend time with their children.

The first few weeks in another country can be exciting, but then the culture shock sets in. This is when you really need a friend. Get out and meet as many good people as you can. You will want friends who see their glass as half-full. The other kind just drags you down.

Children, too, thrive and survive, and they can quietly mourn the loss of friends and extended family. They were part of their identity, who they were, and now they are a world away. Children also suffer the exuberance or deadening of sensory overload. They face almost all the challenges adults' face. Gregarious children may develop introspective tendencies; quiet, measured children may exhibit aggressiveness. They are trying to make sense of it all too! There is no 'one response fits all' model. They have fallen down the rabbit hole with Alice. They will get to the tea party, and given time, they will adapt and grow. Keeping 'home from home' patterns will ease their way. 'Friday night movie time' can be 'Friday night movie time' anywhere! A hug a day can keep the strangeness at bay too! And not just for children!

LIVING IN THE ZONE but which zone?

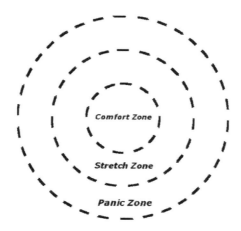

Figure 1: Zone living

It is a brave and bold thing you have done; an exciting and challenging move; a difficult and meaningful move. There are times in those first few weeks where it will all seem too much but you keep going anyway, then something tips and it becomes commonplace for a while. You have adjusted. Then unexpectedly, you are jolted by homesickness. Experience puts this time around the six week mark, although it can be earlier or later – and it can be experienced more than once in the first year. And it can be experienced similarly in subsequent moves! What's going on? You are changing inside. You are learning to make 'foreign' normal.

Looking back you can identify times in your life when you were doing great. You were managing well. You were living the plateau life, maybe high plateau life, but plateau life no less. The ripples in your pond were within your capabilities. This area is often called your Comfort Zone. It can be drawn as a large circle to represent your life, or a small circle, depending on how high a priority it is in your life to be comfortable at any one point in time.

Comfort Zone indicators include:
- Regular routines
- Laid back
- Stuck
- Take few chances
- In control
- Fear of change, to name a few

You stretch yourself to take on something new. This is how you learn. You move away from your Comfort Zone into your Stretch Zone. Each individual's Stretch Zone is different. What might be a huge challenge to me may be easy for you. You give yourself permission to make your Stretch Zone as big or as small as you want. There is no right or wrong in the size of these zones. You are familiar with your Stretch Zone already. You lived in it every time you learned something new. What is left is to decide how big you want to make it this time. It is a normal outcome of moving to a new culture that you live in your Stretch Zone for an extended period of time.

Stretch Zone indicators include:
- Chance/risk taking
- Desire to learn

- Unsettledness in routine
- 'Grass is always greener' attitude
- Steep learning curves
- Buzz factor, to name a few

You may even push yourself beyond your Stretch Zone into your Panic Zone. In fact, you may go straight from your Comfort Zone into your Panic Zone at the speed of light! But whatever the reason or reasons that catapulted you there, it is not somewhere in which you should spend excessive periods.

Panic Zone indicators include:
- Increased stress levels
- Frustration
- Heightened anxiety
- Overeating
- Problem drinking
- Sexual inadequacy
- Weight gain
- Weight loss
- Inability to be alone
- Anti-social behaviour
- Incomplete work
- Need to gossip, again, to name a few

You will often see these Zones represented as closed circles. I draw them with broken circles because I believe that we dip regularly from one to the other depending on what activity you are engaged in. This visual depiction provides a security blanket to people who hesitatingly move away from their Comfort Zone. Visually they have affirmed that they have not passed a solid barrier of no return. In fact, they can often 'see or feel' their Comfort Zone expanding with them which is very powerful.

This is a fluid illustration. It is easy to visualise the circles expanding and contracting depending on choices; obstacles encountered; challenges successfully completed at work and at home; in fact, anything you identify as a success or a challenge.

ZONE CHECK

Take a few minutes to recognise where you are right now:

- Are you in your Comfort Zone?
- Are you moving towards your Panic Zone?
- How big is your Stretch Zone?

Now:

- Draw three concentric circles to represent your Zones.
- Choose a different colour for each Zone.
- While colouring each in, review your choices around each Zone.
- Redoing this exercise regularly will help you identify those tipping moments that move you unexpectedly between Zones.

NOTES on the use of colours:

- Note the colours you use. Are they the same each time for each Zone? Do they differ in lightness or depth?
- Surround yourself with your Comfort Zone and Stretch Zone colours. Perhaps you can use your Comfort Zone colours in your living space and your Stretch Zone colours in your workspace?
- Minimise your Panic Zone colour palette in your life and surroundings.

You now have a firm picture of where you are currently. So what has upset your routine? What event or person has tipped you into the unknown in your new culture? Can you use it for good? Or do you need to manage this out of your life? Again, there is no right or wrong choice; only one that works best for you.

7

EPILOGUE: TO GO OR NOT TO GO

IS IT POSSIBLE to feel trapped in a choice? Yes, it is. I felt trapped from the word go. Trapped in the prospect of staying and trapped in the process of going. And it was an agreed choice. An exciting opportunity but the feelings were there nonetheless and were hard to reconcile. I always felt feeling trapped belonged in the glass-half-empty category and I was wrong, thankfully. Being trapped belongs in the glass-half-empty category; feeling trapped can happen to anyone anywhere regardless of circumstances. And I certainly felt trapped, or its less malign boxed-in cousin, in the lead up to my big moves and in the first weeks and months in a new culture. It's like being in a change-funnel where you bring everything you are to the table and by choice you allow yourself to be dumped in the mouth of that tunnel to be squeezed through a process what will allow you to expand the other end as a new product. I had chosen this funnel which now excludes every other funnel. Some of those will look more enticing as I get close to going over the top on my one. And I become unsure about whether I'll be able to make it or not. I don't know what's ahead but I do know me. I jump.

It begins with a desire to do more with my life; to be all that I can be. I am a lifelong learner, both academic and in the pursuit of knowledge in what it's all about, the big questions of love, life and leaving a legacy. But I am also a creature of habit; I like my Comfort Zone, have so much I want to do in my Stretch Zone and ultimately spend more time in my Panic Zone than is good for my exercise regime. I believe in shared goals in my marriage while holding fast to the need for personal development. We can all be better people. It is my plan that the me you meet tomorrow will be better than the one sitting writing this now. And every new culture move I have made has had at its heart my whole family. Sometimes it may not have looked that way as you can only know the heart of another when it is shared. Looking back works too but that takes time.

Our decision as a couple to leave the UK and live and work in Tokyo was not a difficult one. We had created this opportunity by deciding we had done all we could do in our positions in the UK and it was time for the treat-challenge of going abroad. It felt right; and the money added up. There is nothing wrong in making the money add up in a new post; anything less is underselling yourself and over time you may well come to believe in a less-able you. Of course there may well be other equally important choice-factors other than money; you will need to keep these at the forefront of your mind throughout your posting though as somehow once these have been achieved, for example, fresh air, money will slide silently up the consideration bar and you may find yourself resenting doing the same job in this new place for less money and forget about how much healthier you are as a result. We were excited about the prospect of living in such an amazing place with the money to enjoy it. We could now do all this exciting travel as a family, and we did. This was a no-brainer; something my husband and I had talked *about in college while still boyfriend/girlfriend. Our dreams were moving along.*

Our decision to leave swung us into organisation mode and the logistics of that almost unmade us financially. We had no idea moving overseas could be so expensive. Our daughter was still in University and our son had just finished A Levels and had a gap year planned which he still wanted to do and which we fully supported. It meant us travelling away from our grown up children to live on our own, initially in Tokyo. It was a reverse leaving the nest moment. And it was incredibly hard. I still cannot recall waving goodbye to the two of them at Heathrow Airport without feeling the separation pain intensely. No amount of good things about our new adventure helped assuage the sorrow of that parting that lasted for years clear in my memory and my heart. We each felt it deeply in our own way. I arrived at our destination broken inside, disconnected from those I love deeply yet with a partner I love deeply too. It was so hard not to blame him for what I felt. It was even hard to stand back and even consider what he felt. So we began our dream work experience in a vacuum, one we glossed over and got on with it. That what doesn't kill you makes you stronger, right? Actually, it does, but there's a lot of self-work to do until you finally get there.

Despite the separation pain there was the initial self-satisfied 'I did it' moment as I disembarked in Tokyo. It was nice. It was a validation that I can do more than I thought possible, a moment to savour, an achievement that was dreamlike. There was another moment when I stood in our new home. This was more real, more concrete; another milestone along the new road; a family anchor in a strange place. It was actually happening now; our new life had begun. I was in my new circumstances looking at my new, chosen environment through my life-up-'till-now filter. I was exhausted, sweaty, and hungry. But deep down I knew I had done the right thing. Now it was time to get on with our new living.

I had many "I did it' moments since that first one in Tokyo but it stands out in particular in my memory like a benchmark of sorts, a marker in the sand that other subsequent 'firsts' would be compared to or bolstered up by. My first earthquake experience was another, that too, in Tokyo, plus the myriad other new experiences that were to imprint this foreign culture in my mind like no other before. Language difference played a large part in this. And that was without factoring in critical first impressions while severely jet lagged. I was living well inside my Panic Zone, my neck on swivel each time I left our house. And with my Panic Zone came fear; good helpings of disempowerments; and high levels of anxiety which I strove to conceal. The learning curve was so steep those first few days which is strange to consider because what I was learning was just how to survive physically and emotionally; how to identify grocery products; how to adjust the aircon; to remember the route home. The pull between excitement and stress went on for weeks adjusting down in ferocity with each passing day, with each passing successful benchmark. It was different for each of us. My husband had work related commitments from the word go which included home-language contact. That was hard for him in a different way and it took longer for him to get to know the environs. For me, I had to make my own way like a reverse analogy of a Lilliputian in the land of Gulliver, or so it felt initially. And it was about feelings, and perceptions too. I was trying to make sense of it all through my home-country filter; it was all I had. But bit by bit I lived the new culture way of doing things, of living, and I could feel myself adapting, changing, and settling in. The excitement remained while the anxiety faded. I had learned to cope.

Along the way I had moments of panic when I couldn't cope anymore. These were the 'what have I done' moments when I looked longingly back to what I had left behind and looked with apprehension forward along the timeline of my contract and honestly felt like I couldn't stand another moment. At the flick of a switch what I was doing became too much especially when I was boxed-in by choice in this wonderful opportunity. There were moments of total immersion too; I just couldn't consider another cultural difference, face another rice dish. But these too faded with familiarity and habit. And they mostly occurred anyway when I was physically exhausted. Getting enough good sleep is crucial to the success of any new move.

Note:

In subsequent moves I was able to identify patterns in adjusting culturally and make some interesting observations when returning to a previous other-language environment which I speak more about in **Expat Life: Carousel Moves.** But it is useful to know what to expect generally here keeping in mind that individual responses to a chosen challenge are unique but enough similarities do exist so we can learn from each other.

The first six weeks provide an immense learning curve in your chosen other culture. When you bear in mind that we are all culturally determined by our home experience, programmed to fit into our home culture from birth; this is what we may recognise as our Comfort Zone. Any new move abroad will be compared to this initially, and maybe always, depending on formative experience. It is then reasonable to expect that any choice to live abroad will result in living in your Stretch Zone or Panic Zone for some time. That some-time is personally dependent on how well you can cope and how much you want to cope. Your cultural immersion is also dependent on who you surround yourself with. As an Irish person, if I immerse myself in the Irish abroad to the exclusion of locals then I am reinforcing my Irish nationality as a priority. What I take away locally is similar to an extended holiday experience with friendly natives.

In my move to Tokyo my home-culture was already reinforced by English culture from my many years living and working there, and raising our family there. I was westernised. I had already adjusted my west-of-Ireland farming background to city living. I had some confirmed success at adapting. Tokyo, and Japan, is completely different from Mayo and London. That was a large part of the attraction which I had now to come to living, and working, terms with. At first, everything was strange but I expected that. Not everything was wonderful. I expected that too. But there is a world of difference between expecting and experiencing. This point of difference is what makes travel so transformational; what you experience becomes part of you forever.

In the first few days, in some cases hours, I experienced sensory overload many times. My brain was working overtime trying to fit Japanese cultural norms into my western mindset. In those first few days most did not fit at all. Chopsticks, humidity, wear any colour you like as long as it's black, bowing, taking off my shoes, business men asleep on benches with their briefcases and phones untouched beside them, being pushed onto trains, the fish market, undying politeness, just to name a few – I had no previous experience, no hanger in my cultural closet to hang these hats on. To adapt, I had to go with the flow. Copying living the Japanese way became my first priority. Only then did living there make sense. I had to let go of my knife-and-fork culture. Within six weeks I was able to feed myself reasonably well using chopsticks or at least I was visiting McDonalds less and less. I was feeling confident again. I was proactive. Though bowing on the phone came much later I had the feeling I had arrived.

Then one day I was walking happily home from work when the strangeness set in. Without warning my brain became fixated on my home culture and represented my surroundings to me similar to the day I had arrived. I was devastated. I was homesick. I felt like all the positive, enjoyable culture adapting progress I had built up had been for nothing. I was like a rabbit caught in the headlights of a strange vehicle waiting to run me down while my home car stood at the *roadside with the door open for me. Everything inside me was saying I didn't belong in my new place. I needed to go home. I was close to tears.*

I didn't know it that first time around but this was simply my home culture questioning if I really was ok about changing over to the new one. It's like when you are standing on those diving blocks for the first time really excited to be that far along in training and you hear this whisper in your ear asking you if you're mad to even consider diving from this height. Or all the training you put in to preparing for a marathon only to face that moment of indecision the night before or at the start line. It's an inbuilt survival mechanism. It gives us a moment of clarity, a moment of conscious decision that we can own rather than bumbling along and wondering how we got here at all. Once we recognise this weird moment for what it is we can acknowledge thankfully the survival instinct that has kicked in and move on with our new cultural immersion. Our home-culture acquiesces and we let the new culture in. The one we focus the most on grows stronger; the other fades. We may not be dual citizens but we carry increasingly dual-cultures inside us. We truly globalise ourselves from the inside out.

'The road to success is not straight.

There is a curve called Failure,

A loop called Confusion,

Speed bumps called Friends,

Red lights called Enemies,

Caution lights called Family.

You will have flat tyres called Jobs,

But if you have a spare called Determination,

An engine called Perseverance,

A driver called Willpower,

You will make it to a place called <u>SUCCESS</u>.'

Unknown

PART 2
FAMILY MATTERS

"We are a strange little band of characters trudging through life sharing diseases and toothpaste, coveting one another's desserts, hiding shampoo, borrowing money, locking each other out of our rooms, inflicting pain and kissing to heal it in the same instant, loving, laughing, defending and trying to figure out the common thread that bound us all together."

Emma Bombeck

8

PROLOGUE: FAMILY MATTERS

AT THE HEART of **Family Matters** is that family's matter. To have a successful expat posting a spouse or partner has got to come first followed closely by accompanying children and non-accompanying children. Parents, siblings and extended family take a secondary place. But the truth is that job matters compete for available space, all available space if you let it. Jobs always put demands on personal time regardless of where you are on the ladder. Time and expertise is exchanged for benefits, for the expat package. First and foremost, you are living and working abroad to benefit yourself. Of course you will also want to provide value for money to your employer. It is a natural focus.

There are three main areas to be juggled when moving abroad with your family. In order of importance, these are:

1. **Focus 4 Family**: your family is your crown in life. It is made up of many jewels of different shapes and colour. Your spouse takes centre stage. All of them enhance who you are. You are defined by them and alongside them, and sometimes, in spite of them. Family success brings deep and lasting feelings of achievement. You hold up the world together. With focus, your

family lights up the world for you and for each other. Lack of focus means each jewel is dimmed. What lights are you following?

2. **Care 4 Children**: your children are part of you whether accompanying you or not. They will need sustained focus to ensure a move is truly beneficial for all. More money can mean minders while you work to make more money. But your children are your only true legacy in this world. Who gets to spend the most time with them? What, to you and them, is quality time? What is best for them individually? What are you missing out on?

3. **Wisdom 4 Work**: work is ever expanding. There is no end to the tasks that can make a good venture ever better, a project more productive. It is easy to get sucked in to the exciting and fast-paced work environment where you are constantly validated and your ego is stroked. You become indispensable. Nobody can do this job better than you. And since you are getting paid so well you feel you can go the extra mile. Then the extra mile becomes the norm and suddenly you are rarely home and important milestones in your personal family life pass you by because you have become too busy. Or has your focus changed by choice? What are you gaining by working so much? Where does the tipping point lie between productive and enjoyable work and happy family times and totally immersive work and family alienation? The good news, once informed, you get to choose.

Part 2 explores the challenges and issues faced by modern expats as they seek to enhance their life by working abroad, away from their home culture and comfort base. Most families have survived the transition successfully. Some have returned. Others have broken up and gone their separate ways. Going abroad is not a recipe for success for a marriage that is already in difficulty. Nothing is static. The only constant is change. Being informed helps you make better choices. Going to live abroad is a definite occasion where ignorance will not bring bliss. For those who hold their family close, living and working abroad is the adventure of a lifetime for all.

9

TRAILING SPOUSES, ACCOMPANYING PARTNERS

TRAILING SPOUSE IS an emotional term. In the first instance it conjures up the visual picture of the man striding forward, a harassed wife hurrying along in high heels in his wake often picking up fallen items he has recklessly discard. In a politically correct moment the picture morphs into a suited female striding forward, her husband struggling to carry her excess baggage in her shadow. There is, as yet, no universal set placement for same-sex couples. Whatever the mental image, 'trailing spouse' defines a move where one partner takes the lead; the couple move on the strength of his or her job. The 'trailing spouse' relinquishes financial independence. This loss is recognisably linked to a subsequent dip in self-esteem.

Today, a trailing spouse will either follow or accompany their partner. The language used is important. 'Following' indicates dependency; 'accompanying' an equal opportunity move in work terms. In reality, life is never so clear cut but there is value in exploring where the semantics take us. Following can often lead to a culture of blame: 'I gave up everything to follow you out here! It's all your fault!' Accompanying holds the idea that 'We're in this together' and helps retain the self-identity that is often lost in following. I have met very successful and happy 'followers' and very depressed 'accompanying' partners, and vice versa. So what are the recognisable characteristics of each?

FOLLOWING PARTNERS

These are a magnificent group of people. They are supporters and enablers. This is the group of that old saying, 'Behind every successful man, is a woman!' Gender models have now changed and it is equally as true to repeat the saying now as, 'Behind every successful woman, is a man!' or whatever combination works for you. Professionally, I believe a person is successful on their own merit but the saying just reminds us to continually appreciate our partners for their unfailing personal support. Whatever the circumstances, this group believes in, and acts on, self-sacrifice. They may not share the mover's vision. They may be supporting the person rather than the plan. A picture would represent them walking into the sunset one following in the other's footsteps. But support they do. All the way. There are many reasons for this.

- This is a role they have built for themselves over the years. It is inside their comfort zone. They have no wish to change, and that is ok.
- They are used to being looked after.
- They genuinely find their self-worth fully expressed and valued through this role.
- Their qualifications, if they have any, are not recognised in their new destination.
- The language barrier is too severe for them to work in their new local environment.
- They are not entitled to a work visa.

- There are gender barriers to work.
- They have health needs that impact on their mobility, work span, etc.
- They have young family to look after.
- They have a mobile business of their own, e.g. writer, web designer, etc. to name a few

In an expat move, the expectation often is that the financial package will be better than that had previously so you can be more indulgent in your leisure time. Imagine, as a following partner, having more discretionary time and more money to spend. What a wonderful congruence! While definitely exciting, and if the opportunity presents itself, and this is what you want, do enjoy it, but time will tell very quickly if you have the temperament to do the lunch rounds, the bridge circle, the tennis club, the designer shops ad infinitum without slowly going mad! Alternatively, you can max up the credit card as revenge for the amount of time you spend alone and you begin to believe that this is the only life you could ever, ever countenance. These are dangerous, fragile states. Look to your self-worth. Look to your relationship. Do have an outbreak of common sense. Use what is available to your benefit. Watch out for the hollow moments in your circle. They may be pointing you on to better things.

But what if you follow your partner and the money does not go far enough. He or she is working long hours in stimulating company and you are alone all day, and on a shoestring budget. This is a recipe for hell on earth in your chosen destination. Do your figures carefully. Money does matter in this foreign place; more so here that when you were at home. Talk to your partner. There are many fruitful ways to spend your time that does not involve money. And begin now to plan your way out of this situation. If it is not viable now, it most certainly will not be in six months' time. Plan before you have to.

ACCOMPANYING PARTNERS

These are also a magnificent group of support people. They enable and support by walking alongside their partners and they expect the same back. This back-expectation is a major difference from 'following'. It goes beyond the personal caring within the relationship. Everything is funnelled through this expectation and as a result, more options are explored, even before the initial job offer is accepted. They go with the expectation that both will work or will benefit equally from this chosen posting. It is a clearly defined win-win for both from the outset. A picture would represent them walking hand in hand into the sunset. One may well have a better expat package than the other. It is likely that they will have moved on the strength of one package with the plan for the other person to get work when they get there. They share a joint vision. What might differentiate them from the following partner?

- They both hold qualifications that are recognised in their new country.
- They both believe that they are equally employable.
- They both want to work in their new country. For many professionals, this goes deeper than a wish list. They may work in an area that continuously upskills, and if they are out of the workplace for a set period of time, they will find it difficult to be reemployed.
- They will not have a work visa unless they have interviewed and accepted a job but getting one through a new job is not seen as an obstacle, just logistics.
- They will not have accompanied their partner unless there was a good chance they could get suitable employment or be upskilled.
- They have transferrable skills.

- They are willing and excited about the possibility of retraining or upskilling.
- They are practiced in overcoming barriers to their ongoing success.
- They have high self-esteem.
- They want to learn, again, to name a few

This couple's initial experience in their new environment looks exactly like that of the leader and follower. They both:

- Attend the trans-cultural training delivered by the new business for its staff
- Take part in the social events set up for familiarisation and networking
- Set up the family home
- Establish the domestic routine
- Establish the shopping routine
- Deal with domestic staff
- Take language lessons

But here the similarities end. The 'follower' will see this new routine as their role for the duration; the partner who 'accompanies' will see it as building a sustainable routine upon which they will extend their career. Expectations and perceptions differ. One will settle to the routine; the other will look for opportunities. Quality of life may be measured similarly for both. What is important is for each individual to live their choice and not be overwhelmed, underwhelmed or unduly influenced by those of others. There is no right or wrong here. But one thing for sure – expat life is full of opportunities. Some will fall into your lap; others will present with a gentle enquiry; and there will be those you choose to fight for. Do what you like with them. Ultimately this NOW is your life.

ISOLATION - IT'S LIKE EARLY RETIREMENT

There are startling similar experiences with early retirement and the trailing spouse scenario. If anything, the trailing spouse scenario is more isolated. You are removed from your family, work and social networks as an expat. There is much recognition of the harmful effect of retirement, when one is suddenly isolated from the meaningful work and financial reward cycle that has sustained self-esteem and a home for years. Unless one moves after retirement, one's family dynamic remains constant, as does one's social circle. But as an expat trailing spouse you lose all three instantly. Culture challenges are one thing; isolation is another. It affects every expat. Common indicators are:

- Filling every hour with activity however beneficial or inane.
- An inability to be by oneself.
- Withdrawal from all but family.
- Complete or varying lack of enthusiasm for new environment.
- Forcing a 'glass half full' mentality when inside the bottom has disappeared from the glass.
- A deep, aching loneliness.
- Fear of the unknown.
- Difficulty in getting out of bed in the morning.
- Staying up late watching TV/ movies.
- Alcoholism.
- Smoking.
- Drug abuse.
- Infidelity.
- Blaming others.
- Weight gain.
- Weight loss.
- Excessive behaviour.

- Other. Take the time to identify your personal indicators. Seek help if the emotional undercurrents are threatening to swallow you.

'I was a trailing spouse for our four years in Shanghai. I accompanied my husband and was offered paid employment in my then professional work area, IT. However, I declined for two reasons: I couldn't work at my desired level because I didn't have the language to do so; and the pay I was offered subsequently was not congruent with my level of expertise. Regardless of cultural differences, I know my worth and I find it deeply offensive this practice of bargaining from the lowest common denominator. I decided to retrain. My personal philosophy is that if I am not working, I am learning. Our financial package allowed me this freedom. This was the only time I lived the 'trailing spouse' life.

An experienced expat of twenty years, I didn't anticipate the isolation challenges I was to face. My husband left for work at 6.30am. I closed the door behind him and the day loomed before me, mine to fill as I pleased. Exciting? Yes! Sustainable? No! I need someone to talk to. I began to feel disconnected from life around me; that wasn't difficult, in fact, I think it's to be expected along the expat journey. But the troubling thing was that I didn't really want to do anything about it not only initially but time and again!

The reality was, in the beginning, everyone I knew was part of his work organisation. As the boss's wife, I was treated with a certain deference. It was difficult to build a friendship within his work body; not everyone could separate us as individuals and it became onerous to watch every 'p' and 'q'. Whether we liked it or not, we reflected on each other. We are a very private couple and I couldn't be myself with this group until I knew whom I could trust. And even if it was obvious they all worked anyway! I needed company during the day not in the evenings and weekend.

I found it extremely difficult not having my own income. I struggled with feelings of inadequacy as I felt I wasn't contributing to our marriage. I hated withdrawing money from the ATM with his card. I do it now but it has taken me four years to be comfortable with it. I tried to organise our weekend schedule so we pass an ATM and he withdraws the money. Now, I have no problem with paying the bills with his card; it's just money for my personal stuff I struggle with. For example, he can get a haircut for 50RMB; my trip to the hairdresser is in excess of 500RMB. When I was working for a monthly pay check I wouldn't think twice about it. The thing is, I would have no problem if the shoe was on the other foot. I would expect him to use my card in the same was he naturally expects me to use his. It was an eye-opener for me as to how much of my self-esteem was invested in the monthly pay check. It can be distinctly disempowering to live as a trailing spouse if you are used to paying your way.

I was astounded to find I needed a valid reason for getting out of bed! Once the excitement of the initial move wore off, it was very clear that this situation needed to be managed. Despite my courses, the gym outside the door, the exciting city at my fingertips, I had great difficulty mustering up the energy to do anything. I had reached saturation level for seeing new sights. I wasn't sure I wanted to invest in another friendship that would dissolve when we moved again. Depression lurked around the corner despite my being a self-starter. It was hard, hard, hard, being a trailing spouse. It was hard listening to his busy day, empathising and encouraging, when I was breathing empty on so many levels. It took a decided effort not to live vicariously through

> Expat life is full of demanding, exciting, challenging, empowering and disempowering, needy, controlling people. It validates you. It builds you up. It sucks you dry. At the heart of all these experiences are vulnerable souls longing for meaningful connection.

him. That's when I decided to take my laptop and study and write for a couple of hours a day in Starbucks or Costa. Having that outside focus was crucial.

I have always been happy in my own company. I can spend occasions within a crowd or with some few friends too. I am family orientated; both of our children are married to wonderful partners so we're a single couple again although we'll always happily be parents. In twenty years of expat living and working I had never experienced anything like the isolation that came with being a trailing spouse! For me the choices were: I could wallow and fade from the story of my own life and blame my husband for it all or I could reinvent myself, begin a new career, and build value out of the emptiness. I had to go way down to see that, and let go of some of my IT dreams. Some changes were easy and some hard but I did it! And, guess what? There's plenty of room and time for all my dreams. I always ask: Am I a better person for this experience, this journey? I make the answer 'yes'.'

Expat life is full of demanding, exciting, challenging, empowering and disempowering, needy, controlling people. It validates you. It builds you up. It sucks you dry. At the heart of all these experiences are vulnerable souls longing for meaningful connection. That connection is with people not a country. I came here in support of my husband; we live here because he supports me. HR Departments do a wonderful job logistically for their foreign workers. But where is the emotional support? The counselling? The mediation for when relationships break down? There are often Helplines run on volunteer, charity lines. And many big businesses are beginning to recognise that they may need to look out for the emotional and psychological needs of their workers too. Talk about this with your partner. Above all, keep the channels of communication open. Make a commitment to listen to each other actively. Quality time can be had in and around even the most frenetic work situations. Set up a code word or phrase to use when reaching overload. Choose your social events with care. It is ok to say 'No' to an invitation. Remember, you are always on show wherever you go. And protect your private time vigorously. You came to this place sharing a dream with your partner. Do you want to leave together?

TRAILING SPOUSE MATTERS

- Know your personality type. Are you a self-starter or a self-saboteur?
- Decide before you leave if you are going to live in your new country or just put in time.
- Do you share your partner's vision or are you ok about supporting it regardless of personal cost?
- What exactly do you want from your working partner in terms of support?
- What do you think he or she wants from you?
- Keep talking! This is not the best place to continue a sulking habit or begin one. I have yet to meet a mind-reader. I had hoped after 35 years of marriage that my significant other might have just grasped the basics but no, he hasn't. He is just as perplexed now as when we first got married when I act out of character. Happily, these are only few occasions usually related to a stress reaction.
- Know what sets you off! Minimise those occasions as much as possible.
- Are you a jealous person? Why? Is the insecurity yours or your partners? Trust is crucial in expat moves.
- Do you continue to look after yourself? Your partner is working every day with professionally groomed people. You can be casual but don't be a slob.
- Are you there regularly for your partner at the end of the day? How are you going to have a relationship if you're never there? If you're always out enjoying yourself on their card? Does your working partner make any effort at all? Do you have date nights? Or are all the nice meals out on the business card with the business people?
- Choose where you live carefully in your new country. Choose for the way you both like to live not for the perceived 'house for the boss'. No matter how beautiful the four walls that surround you are, they will be your cage, your prison, unless you have a way of interacting with others that relieves your isolation.

- Internet access is crucial. It can be hard keeping in touch with family and friends in a different time zone but it can be a life saver.
- Try out all the groups you can. You will find a kindred spirit one day.
- Reach out to contacts via email or text. Other expats will usually be delighted to help you out. I found a wonderful friend that way. Would you believe it, we had gone to the same university at the same time twenty-five years earlier but we studied different disciplines so our paths never crossed.
- Consider charity work. Even the seasonal events can be a happy congruence of your emotional needs with helping those less fortunate than you. Meeting like-minded people, and working alongside them on an altruistic project, is very fulfilling. It helps put things in perspective.
- Consider learning the language. This will help you access the culture more and make ordinary life easier.
- Consider learning some specific cultural crafts and skills. This will help you integrate culturally.
- Take a course, a diploma, a Masters or Doctorate. Upskill yourself so you leave in a better position for the next move.
- Plan at least a day ahead, and actually do something every second day.
- And do shower every single day! Look after you!

10

ACCOMPANYING CHILDREN

ACCOMPANYING CHILDREN, NON-ACCOMPANYING children, grandchildren, pregnancy, future children, miscarriages, abortion, IVF, divorce, remarriage, anything to do with children needs to be explored thoroughly before accepting a post abroad. Additionally, marrying a foreigner requires open and frank discussion about subsequent extended family visits and involvement. It would be wonderful if these discussions provided an ideal, workable solution that stands the test of time. Unfortunately, it rarely is so; as situations and opportunities open up, parents need to be proactive in renegotiating any deal that will continue to provide the best care and provision for all involved.

ACCOMPANYING CHILDREN

Consider the following carefully when moving with children:

- Age
- Gender

- One parent working in new post
- One parent working away from home on their own
- Both parents working
- Child minder
- Nursery
- Schooling
- Out of school curriculum
- Outside facilities
- Safety
- Transport
- Special needs – health, learning, etc.

There are several age ranges that warrant a closer look when moving abroad: babies, toddlers and pre-schoolers, primary school pupils, middle school students, senior school students, university undergraduates, and university post graduate students. All of these can accompany parents on their expat journey legally as long as they are supported by their parent or parents in situ. Many companies will support the education of children from primary school to undergraduate level. This is a significant financial commitment from your company. It is likely that this will provide a psychological lock-in to your contract unless you find a similar deal. Some companies even cover university and other training opportunities for a trailing spouse. What a great opportunity! Some, though, cover the bare minimum or offer nothing at all. Read the small print carefully and do not be afraid to open a negotiation with your prospective employer on this matter. But do it before you sign your contract. Anything subsequent to that is goodwill.

BABIES: Many people say that taking on a significant expat package while you have babies is the best. It means a parent can take time off to be with the baby while the other brings in what can often be more than they both realised in their previous jobs. Alternatively, it can mean they you can now afford a nanny to look after your baby while you both work. In between scenarios include part-time nanny, part time home-help or full time both with only one parent still working. Whatever the arrangement it is seen as a big assist to the young mother or father, whoever has taken on the parenting role full time. While the advantages are obvious the disadvantages are less clear. Some things to consider if you find yourself heading into this way of living for the first time:

- How will you deal with others around your home all the time?
- Will your new staff speak your language? How will you communicate with them if they don't?
- How trained are they? Do you agree with the way they do things?
- Are you happy sharing your baby?
- How will you feel if your baby responds more lovingly to them than you?
- How will you deal with misunderstandings at the personal level? While you may be a wonderful manager and mediator at work, these close-up and personal interactions are a different thing altogether. Here you are deeply emotionally invested in the outcome.
- If you are working full time also, are you happy with your baby being brought up according to the cultural and language norms of your nanny? How will you agree discipline? How much actual time will you both as parents spend with your baby? While extra money will provide a more comfortable home, no compensatory elements can fill in for time missed with your child.

TODDLERS: When you move with toddlers, it can be a blessing to have that extra pair of hands around to look after him or her, particularly if you have a lively kinesthetic child. Parenting roles can be more clearly defined with the nanny and by this stage you may well be considering doing something for yourself now that the 24/7 dependency has eased. Issues here revolve around discipline and language acquisition. Be clear with your nanny how you wish your child to be disciplined. Make sure your child respects your wishes and those of your nanny also. Your nanny may well not discipline if it is not according to her known ways of doing so. She may be afraid she will get sacked if she does not get it right. Her future work depends on a good reference from you so she will not wish to rock the boat. She may well have left a young family of her own to look after yours. Language acquisition is tremendously important at this stage. Your toddler will focus on the sounds around him or her, discarding those that are not in accordance with what he or she hears; their palette is formed in this pre-school stage. All babies have the ability to learn whichever language or languages surround them. Have you ever noticed how babies all make the same sounds? Then five years later they are speaking their mother tongue fluently? The best outcome is a true bilingualism; that of you and your nanny. If you are both working, make sure one of you gets home early enough to talk to your child so he or she hears your language as often as that of the nanny.

PRE-SCHOOLERS and **KINDERGARTEN** children are entering the social aspect of living and learning. They begin to spend more and more time in the extended environment of other children and less in the singular, selfish, home environment. They learn to share; some do this effortlessly while others have a real struggle in sharing. They learn as much by observing and interacting with others at this stage as the formal element of schooling they encounter. In single-child families, this interaction is crucial to normal development. As an expat, you may have more choice in terms of early schooling or you may have less. By there is a better chance that you will have the money to choose. This is something you will have already discussed into the move equation a few years earlier. Explore all options. Spend time in your prospective school environment. Do the children look happy? Is the environment properly ventilated or warm? Does the staff look happy? What is the child:teacher/carer ratio? Has the pre-school or kindergarten got any recommendations? Do they have a wait list? Speak to parents if possible. How long a journey will it be for your child? Will your nanny take him or her? Will your driver? Will you keep employing your nanny? Who will pick up and look after your child if they are sick and you are now working or have a full social calendar?

CASE STUDY 1: Martin writes

Sara (not her real name) was a three-year-old preschooler who joined an international school midway through the year. Her family background is Chinese but she was born in Italy and speaks Italian. Clearly the first few days of school for her were confusing, not least because she was hearing a third language for the first time and it was being used throughout the day. Her parents supported her in the initial days and in timely fashion withdrew to allow her to find her feet. This she did in an impressively short period. Teachers worked well with her in developing her confidence to speak and to begin to interact with her peers. Between January and June she grew into a comfortable, talkative and much-admired member of her class, progressing to the next grade without hesitation from teachers. She is bright but crucially she is young and has a default language (Italian) already established.

PRIMARY/ELEMENTARY: You should begin to look at possible schools for your child as soon as he or she starts pre-school. You may have already chosen to live near your preferred school or your search now may require a home move. Your school choice may well reflect:

- Your nationality. You may be posted overseas for a season and will be returning home within the school life of your child so you are looking for a seamless transfer curriculum-wise.
- Your income. If your job does not cover school fees, you will need to shop around for a best fit.
- Your child's educational needs. Your child may require a gifted school programme; a language intense school programme; a supportive school programme; a high activity sports programme, etc. Your expat financial packet should allow you to explore the opportunities your new environment provides as you build for the future.

There are many different curricula available today internationally. Martin Donnellan, Primary School Principal, International School Florence writes:

When considering the educational milieu which the school-age children of expatriates will possibly encounter, three main strands emerge:

1.   It may be possible for children, fortunately, to continue to study and learn in the curriculum of their native country. A number of countries have established such school outside their territories in areas where there are a significant number of their citizens' resident or where there may be significant trade or commercial interest in developing such a community, school availability being a significant attraction for potential families. The most obvious here is Britain. British schools are ubiquitous across continents and copies of this model also abound. Part of the reason for this is historical from the age of empire but in recent decades there has been a noticeable development of new British schools across the world delivering the English National Curriculum. The popularity of these English language schools can occasionally cause difficulty, as they can be quickly oversubscribed. Early registration is advisable, once families have clarity about a posting. Australia, USA, France, Germany,

Japan, Korea, India, amongst others, also offer mother-tongue schools at select locations across the globe.

2.   Clearly this will not be suitable in all cases. Families may move to a posting where their national curriculum is not available. A second option is the look for the availability of international schools which offer an international programme. The most extensive network of such schools is via the International Baccalaureate Organisation which now has about 4000 schools worldwide and offers three programmes for Primary, Middle and Diploma students from age 3 – 18. This is an English language setup but significant cognizance is taken of the mother tongue of students, it often been included in the curriculum. The attraction of these schools and programmes is in the portability of their curriculum and pedagogy. A student taking the Primary Years Programme in an IBO school in China, for instance, would very quickly acclimatise to a PYP school in the USA or Europe as the language of instruction, pedagogy, inquiry-driven learning and development of the Learner Profile would be the same, though the physical environment might be distinctly different.

3.   Similarly families may look to schools which offer other commercial programmes such as the International Primary Curriculum (IPC) or the Cambridge Primary Curriculum (CPC). These are often British or local schools with a desire to attract English-speaking foreigners as well as a strong representation from their own citizens, and a programme such as these will certainly be attractive locally.

A school should provide:
- A balanced curriculum underwritten by a reputable curriculum authority

- Excellent school leadership
- Qualified staff
- A safe school environment
- Well-resourced library
- Integrated technological teaching
- Broad sports programme
- Indoor and outdoor sports facilities
- Broad arts programme
- Broad musical programme with the ability for private instrumental tuition
- An active Parents Support Group
- A shared learning responsibility with parents.

Your expat packet may cover all expenses or basic tuition, or a percentage of tuition for a second and subsequent child. Know what is already covered, and how it is covered. Does the bill go to your company automatically or do you pay and then get reimbursed? It is likely that you will have to cover the extras yourself.

As a parent you should be prepared to supply all the support your chosen school requires to make this the best learning experience for your child. You will be required to:

- Attend teacher-parent meetings
- Commit to supporting your child in their homework but not doing it for them
- Alert them to any learning issues your child may be temporarily or otherwise experiencing
- Sign the Homework Diary. Let your child's teacher know why your child was unable to finish homework or if it was too easy
- Keep your child in school every day; i.e. not withdraw them without consent
- Get your child to school on time each day
- Collect them promptly at the end of the day

- Keep them in the required uniform
- Support the school in any external testing they may advise within reason.

This is an amazing opportunity for your child. They will often 'catch' your attitude to their new school and respond accordingly. Similarly, they will 'catch' your optimism or pessimism for your new environment. Whatever the home influence, their first day at school will be similar to any first day at school anywhere:

- They will not have slept much the previous night whether from anxiety or excitement.
- They may have a tummy ache from both.
- They may race ahead or cling to you. Be sensitive to your child's feelings. Some actually feel their parents' are abandoning them for good in this place called 'school'. The second day should be better for these children as they have now experienced that they can go home again! Be sensitive to your own feelings. You may well feel abandoned as they race ahead excitedly without a backward glance!

A new expat child who has already been to school before has more to contend with. It is not necessarily the 'school academic' bit that may worry them first but the following:

- They miss their friends. Everyone in the playground or class seems to have a friend but them.
- They may not understand the language spoken by other children or their teacher.
- The school food is different. They feel they should know what to do since they have been to school before but they don't. They may feel disempowered and retreat into themselves or become unusually aggressive. Their grades may suffer as they are not relaxed enough in their new environment to learn well.
- It might be the first time they have been to a multi-cultural school. Other children can look scary.

- The books are different.
- They do things differently.
- They feel stupid in their new school uniform.
- They are scared of their new teacher not liking them because they find remembering their Tables difficult.
- They are so used to having things done for them by their nanny that changing for PE takes too long and they get in trouble.

The best you can do is to be there for your child. Keep talking with them. Share stories. Build friendships with other school parents to support your child's friends-sharing. Listen to what your child is saying and what their body-language is telling you. If the light goes out in their eyes it is time to investigate more and don't be afraid to change schools. You child has only one chance at being eight, nine or ten; and this is it! The impact of moving countries and cultures regularly is dealt with in detail in **Expat Life: Carousel Moves.**

CASE STUDY 2: Martin writes

*By way of contrast to **Case Study 1** I recall two students I encountered at a school in Asia. One was aged twelve and his brother was two years younger. They were at the point of moving from Primary to Secondary school. There was an issue however in that neither had a standard of English which was allowing them to comfortably access the required curriculum in a British school. In this case however both boys did not have a grounding in their mother tongue as they had moved around Asia quite a bit in their young lives. There were unsure of how to communicate in any language, regularly mixing languages and often being quite frustrated at their lack of progress. The lack of parental support and involvement also contributed to their malaise. Curriculum content and pedagogy was immaterial here; rather a fundamental lack of the tools and strategies associated with the development of a* *confident mother tongue left these boys with a significant educational challenge.*

MIDDLE SCHOOL may be a natural extension of a highly successful elementary/primary. It may be on the same campus; if not, it is normally nearby. The entire upper class may be transferring and this can be very comforting or alarming: comforting if your child is doing well with an excellent cohort of students; alarming if there are aspects of non-achievement. As a parent, you are best placed to objectively and personally evaluate the move. If alarming:

Do:

- Talk to your child about his or her fears, anxieties, questions
- Discuss the move with your child's teacher
- Involve the school Principal, if necessary
- Meet your child's middle school tutor
- Talk to other parents whose input you value and respect
- Talk to each other!

Don't:

- Avoid the situation
- Blame your child – 'if you'd studied more . . .'; 'if you weren't friends with . . .'
- Blame the 'old' school – 'it was your job to get ahead of this . . .
- Blame the 'new' school before you even give them a chance.
- Blame your partner for getting you all into this mess in the first place!

If you do not like what you see in the on-site middle school, look around. Beware 'the grass is always greener' attitude though. While you know almost first-hand what the adjoining middle school is like, you may not have all the information on the new school despite your best efforts. And at this stage, it could be your child that is creating the non-achieving situation. He or she is, after all, entering puberty when the brain starts some serious rewiring. It may well be their personal resistance you are picking up on rather than the school's objective outcomes.

Whether as a new expat or a continuing expat student, this is an anxious time for all students. They are moving from top of the primary/elementary pile to the bottom of the middle school pile. Chances are they will be experiencing having subject teachers for everything for the first time. Additionally, they will have to become familiar with their new building as they will now be moving to their teacher's base not the teacher coming to their classroom. They will have to manage lockers; detailed timetable moves; time constraints for getting to class in time; changing rooms; communal, although segregated, showers after sports; dining hall banter and routines. Of all these, it is the showers that cause most angst. Your children's bodies change significantly at this time but not all change at the same pace. Ridicule for what one has, and what one has not, abounds. These refrains exist forever. Chances are you remember your own puberty days; the embarrassment and the jibes. To your child, this is unique and often painful. Sometimes the only way to survive it is to beat the bully at his or her own game. Or, to join a gang. Your teenager will often transfer his or her anger and impotence at school taunters and bullies to you and other siblings when he or she gets home. Your child will be unaware of his or her actions; you too may be unaware of this transference and meet fire with fire. So much of this can be diffused by a simple comment like, 'Bad day then. Want to talk about it?' This is often enough to redirect the course of the evening. Chances are you teenager will voluntary offer an explanation later or will at least engage normally with the family again. Should you prompt for one? Maybe. Play it by ear. You know your child best. Maybe a, 'Let me know if I can help,' is enough

> The choice of school is yours as a parent to do what you know best for your child in your personal circumstances. There will be many people who will offer you an opinion, whether solicited or not, welcome or unwelcome.

for starters. But you should definitely prompt and stay close if your teenager is withdrawn for an unusual amount of time. You are best placed to recognise what an 'unusual' amount of time is.

The choice of school is yours as a parent to do what you know best for your child in your personal circumstances. There will be many people who will offer you an opinion, whether solicited or not, welcome or unwelcome. Many are genuine. They are offering you the knowledge and advice they would have liked to have had in your place. Some will want to coerce you as they seek on-going validation for their own choice. Start your search early enough to give yourself all the time you need to investigate all angles. Do take into account your child's feelings as much as you can. Then own your decision and move on.

Bence, 14, an international student, shares his early experiences of moving from the US to Shanghai:

For me expat life is all about changes. When I first came to China I was immediately bombarded with many smells. Smells like dried fish, tofu, duck etc. That was a huge change for me. I was not only shocked by the strange smells, the people also shocked me. The people are not what you expect them to be like. Most of the people spit anywhere they can and for small babies they cut a hole in the pants and diapers so if a child has to use the bathroom they just do their business anywhere, and by anywhere I mean on metros, public parks, even in stores.

When I started school I was even more shocked by the way the cleaning ladies (Aiyis) clean during the day. Now my definition of cleaning is cleaning the windows, the bathrooms, dusting off dust from shelves, etc., but the Chinese clean one area and one area only. That is the floor. During the day all they do is clean the floor with bleach water, which actually makes it dangerous for the kids. It's as slippery as a skating rink. One last thing that was a change for me was the Chinese sense of humor. They do not understand any sarcasm. They take everything seriously especially the children. That is my expat life.

HIGH SCHOOL is a demanding time for your young adult. The choices they make will define their life from now on, as will their achievements. The tests and checks are for real now. They matter like they have never mattered before. The outcome can influence so many things in later life. The big three challenges often revolve around:

- Academics
- Future choices
- Relationships

Only a very small percentage of young adults at high school level know exactly what they want to do when they graduate. This may be in congruence with a parent's wish for their child's future or not. It's a very happy coincidence if they are. If they are not, there are three possible outcomes for parents:

- Coerce your young adult into the path you want him or her to follow regardless of their wishes. This is often accompanied by a withdrawal of financial support if they do not comply. This is a sure way to build estrangement with your child.

- Support your young adult completely in his or her choice even though you know it is not the best use of their talents. Be prepared to be proven wrong. This is in line with the quote, 'Support the man, if not the plan.' In my experience, while difficult, this builds the base for a continued meaningful relationship with your child.

- Compromise. This is the most often chosen middle ground. Provided you have kept the channels of communication open with your growing young adult, it is likely that you can now have a well-structured discussion about the best direction for the future. He or she is old enough now to acknowledge your reasonable arguments and be able to present his or her opinion clearly. This leads to 'giving something a chance with the possibility of change in the second year of university or training school if your child finds he really is not suited to it.' More options are on the cards. Your young adult has your support and the communication doors are wide open. There is less chance of him or her dropping out and disappearing off the radar.

But before you even get to make these decisions, the question arises as to how much you should influence your child in course choices for high school? And how much you should tutor to the outcome? These are not easy questions, parents all over the world struggle with the possible answers annually. For the expat, there is an almost unspoken expectation that their young adult will proceed to third level education. For high industry jobs a basic degree is a necessity; a further qualification desirable for leadership roles. But high-money jobs can be manual labour posts that have a danger-money pay element for working in inhospitable, dangerously unstable environments. Expat parents are like every other parent in the world in that they want something better for their child or at least, something of the same. Your young adult will need to be directed to a working opportunity that will provide the same level of lifestyle that he or she is experiencing with their parents overseas. This is an interesting conundrum. It has taken you, as parents, several years to climb that worthwhile ladder; your child may not realise the hard work he or she has ahead to realise the same for themselves. They may want something different; something more locally based. One thing is pretty sure as an expat parent – you and your adult children will live apart for considerable stretches, often in different continents. Once upon a time, a long, long time ago, children moved out of the family home and lived an hour down the road. Now, there is the exciting aspect of different country visits and the logistical headaches that can accompany this.

Should you influence your teenager as he or she begins high school? Yes, definitely. You know your teen better than they do themselves. Influence, encourage, take advice from school, and then help your child choose his or her subjects. Schools have core subjects that are a curriculum requirement. Your choices will be around languages, arts, music, sports, and humanities. Should you tutor them within an inch of their lives? No. Somewhere in this two year period your teen needs to take ownership of his or her learning if they have not done so already. They need to become pro-active around their life. You cannot spoon feed them forever. By all means provide some support, if necessary, but if you have to tutor your teen for every math component, for example, maybe it is time to let go of the dream that he or she will be the mathematician of the future.

You may well have the opportunity here to send your teen to boarding school if this is within the financial support from your company. In this case, see the next chapter on non-accompanying children which includes university students too.

During this period your young adult will be exploring relationships in more depth than previously. Do make sure he or she has had proper sex education and knows how to keep themselves, and others, safe. Some expat situations will require abstinence, as may your religious practices. Make sure your young adult knows what appropriate public behaviour is. Other locations will provide more danger of HIV contact and STDs. This is not a time to be coy about such things or to blame them for being irrational. 'Tim Irrational' or 'Kate Irrational' is their new name in the land of hormones! Be prepared to be side-lined for long hours on social media with friends. The exodus from the nest has begun.

ACCOMPANYING CHILD MATTERS

A good expat package will mean you have choices:

- [ ] Additional home support when your children are young. This is often when you need it most.

- [ ] A choice of preschools and kindergartens for your toddler, and a nanny to take her there and back freeing you up to look out for 'you' again.

- [ ] A driver to make the commute easier and safer.

- [ ] A choice of different international curriculum schools for your young child. These fee-paying schools will often have an extended programme your child can benefit from.

- [ ] A choice of middle schools that offer different international curricula with extended after-school programmes.

- [ ] A choice of high schools which offer different international curricula with extra-curricular provision to develop an all-round student.

- [ ] The possibility of your child studying anywhere in the world at university level provided he or she meets any academic and language requirements. This is a truly wonderful global opportunity.

- [ ] Language acquisition itself. How wonderful to lean a new language naturally in its home environment!

There are a few observations below that are meant to have you think twice about taking a post where you will be bringing your children along. It is your choice to decide whether these are deal-breakers. No chapter on accompanying children on an expat posting would be complete without them. Consider:

- [ ] Health issues.

- o Does your child have an existing condition that needs careful medical monitoring? Will this expertise be available on site? For example, does your child have asthma?

- o Do you want to expose your infant/young child to malaria? How restricted will your life be to avoid this? How available is medical aid?
- o What is the highest AQI (Air Quality Index) you are prepared to endure? Should you expose your child to this?
- ☐ Safety.
- o Will you need an armed escort as you move around?
- o Is your environment hostile? Is there a danger of being kidnapped?
- o Can you reconcile to living in an armed compound 24/7?
- ☐ Education.
- o Does your child have special learning needs? Will your new environment be able to support him or her? For example, Asperger's Syndrome
- o Does your child have any special physical needs, for example, spina bifidia? Are schools in your new environment equipped with ramps, wheelchair toilets, etc.
- o Do you require a home language school for your child? Is there one available? Or will you enrol him or her in a mainstream foreign school so she or he can learn that new language? Will you then be happy in the delay in his or her learning while he or she catches up?
- o If you or your partner is doing lots of travelling with your new job, how will it all work out?

The above list is indicative, not exhaustive. Put everything on the table for discussion, positive and negative, before you sign your contract. After you sign, your focus moves to managing outcomes. This is not just about what you can do; it is more about what is the best possible outcome for all.

11

NON-ACCOMPANYING CHILDREN

IT IS NOT unusual to meet expats whose children do not accompany them in their new chosen country. There are a number of reasons why this might be the case:

- Older children. There is currently an increase in the number of older people who take on expat posts, particularly in senior management that require a great deal of expertise. Their children may already be self-sufficient or they are in third level education and elect to remain in situ.

- Undergraduates and post graduates are more likely to remain while their parents go to work abroad.

- Younger students may be attending a boarding school. This is often a preferred schooling option when couples move to work in an inhospitable or dangerous location.

- Children may be with a divorced or separated partner and may not have the option of travelling with the outward bound parent.

- Children of a single parent may be left in the care of grandparents.
- Children may remain with a father or mother while the other travels to work.

Whatever the circumstances, children do find themselves staying 'at home' while their parent or parents are working abroad. This comes from individual 'best' choices. There is no right or wrong way of schooling and providing for your non-accompanying children, only best fit. The ensuing situations often produce an insidious 'more' climate though.

FOR THE PARENT:

- More time apart from children. Non-accompanying children may not be able to appreciate the deep emotional distress this can cause parents. They have enough of their own loss and abandonment issues to deal with.
- More financial demands to meet the new situation. A bottomless purse image comes to mind. Depending on the age and work situation of your non-accompanying children, this can become incredibly expensive eroding most of the financial benefits working away from home bestows. Even if your non-accompanying child is a self-sustaining adult, there is a tendency for older expat parents to compensate for their absence by working out best deals with their children, e.g. letting them live rent free in the family home for a protracted period of time until they get on their feet; providing a car for them; paying for holidays so they can be together, etc.
- More guilt feelings as your drive to self-actualisation and family provision means you are actually doing well, better than in years, yet your children are making do without the full hands-on parenting package. Some non-accompanying children are fine left by themselves for long periods of time; others not so. They may not be able to communicate this

directly to you so keep an eye out for cracks. You will know best what these are for your children.

- More travel time to be with children. You can chalk up a lot of air miles this way. Watch your health. Constant travel is physically draining.

- More money spent on family travel. This often results in an expat parent travelling only for family reasons with no real holiday in years. This needs to be managed carefully so both sides do not begin to feel resentment. Why not converge on a new place together? It is a wonderful opportunity to explore new places as you re-engage with each other. Both of you will have changed; however the focus is normally on the child.

- More speed parenting which resolves into more intense parenting within the short time 'at home'. This is painful. In the short time you have together, you would prefer to have a peaceful, productive time together. However this is often not the case. Maybe the first few days will be idyllic, then the cracks appear. It can be hard challenging the status quo and then leaving again but it is something you must face up to. This is the journey of a lifetime not a 40 minute TV serial episode. Whether you are on site all the time or not, you are still the parent. Distance does not diminish that.

- More estrangement. There is an expected drawing-apart during the teenage years. Leaving to work away from your children can lead to feelings of abandonment which often work out as the child withdrawing from the parents.

- More unsettledness. Instead of your posting bringing you your desired security you find living cross-continent is splitting your focus, energy and emotions. You cannot leave your children fully behind, and neither should you, and you cannot be fully present in your new life.

FOR THE NON-ACCOMPANYING CHILD

- More time left to their own devices. This can be wonderfully freeing and intensely anxious, regardless of age. Growing up is like that anyway but this 'left behind' or 'abandoned' situation will only exacerbate the roller-coaster feelings.

- More blame. It is very common for non-accompanying children to blame their parents and their upbringing for everything that goes wrong in their lives. And things will go wrong as children grow up, make poor choices, and have to deal with the consequences. It happens anyway but in this instance their safety blanket is thousands of miles away. They can feel more vulnerable, and chances are they will lash out in unpredictable ways. They may form unhelpful attachments. Sometimes their poor choice is from a lack of having you in their life or a lack of reflection in the moment.

- More financial draws. I was going to say 'more financial demands' but what happens in practice can be more subtle. Most children get to understand early on that the direct approach can be too aggressive and will normally result in a 'no' outcome. However, if they present a more soft appeal, often from a peer inclusivity approach, they are more likely to get want they want, and a lot more perhaps. Children read their parents clearly; non-accompanying children can be so precise as to be manipulative. Some non-accompanying children can really make their parents pay for leaving them behind.

- More selfishness. Because the non-accompanying child has had to fend for himself, or herself, in a non-traditional manner, often in sharp contrast to their friends or peers, they can often become extremely selfish and judge everything by 'what's in it for me?' They can become intolerant of parent choices in everything from watching the News on TV to proposed holidays. Behind this can be a jealousy of any time the parent does not dedicate to them when they are together. It is as if once they are reunited they have to be joined at the hip. But even that becomes a source of low grade conflict until there is a clearing of the air. It can be really awkward spending time together but it is so well worth the effort. For when the time is taken to dig deep and resolve issues, there is that deep validation and love, and approval and acceptance all around.

Fionnuala writes:

I have always felt close to my parents and, when I was in my final year of university, they broached the subject of them going to work in Japan, I was somewhat shocked and delighted. It was not the first "big move" for them, but it would be the first that would divide our family. During the school year I would often miss the comfort of knowing I could call at any time, or even drop over to see them. I remember a few low moments where the time difference really didn't help. However, above all, I remember sharing their adventure vicariously, and due to the new-found wonders of Skype, I did manage to keep in contact regularly. In fact, the reality of them being overseas eventually presented far more positive things in my life than I perceived at the time. It gave me an open door to see the world, a job prospect after university, and ultimately, the path was laid for me to meet my future husband.

I know in time all things fade, and we tend to have one feeling about a life event surface to be the way we "feel about that event" forever. I have to honestly say that I don't remember the trying times, or loneliness, or separation. Rather I remember that time as an awakening within our family that the world truly IS our oyster, and that we can (and should) go experience new places, cultures and to dream big. For that, I will always be grateful.

THE FAMILY BENEFITS

Handled sensitively, and provided relationships are recognised as two-way streets and worked on accordingly, the benefits of expat living on the whole family can outweigh the struggles by a big margin. They punch in way above the insidiousness of the 'more' culture that develops to one level or another.

- More money can really mean better quality of life for all.

- Travel broadens the mind. More money can provide more travel for everyone involved.

- Money buys better education opportunities. This can be in better schools, better additional opportunities around an already good school, better universities or courses.

- Money can buy a better lifestyle overall. Students can live better, and travel more easily. They can afford the gadgets and gizmos that will enhance their educational and social standing, and the gym membership and new clothes to keep them looking cool! As is often the case with parents all over the world, the children can look amazing while the parents come second. The self-sacrificial drive to put your children first is not diminished by distance; rather it is enhanced many times over as parents strive to make it a win-win situation for all.

- Money can buy more time together in nice places but it is up to the family dynamic if this provides quality time or not.

- Money builds the future. It is possible to pay-it-forward; plan for that business opportunity for retirement or for your adult child.

- Worldwide working and travelling develops perspectives that watching a TV programme cannot. The value that is caught is incalculable. Is the outcome always positive? Not necessarily but mostly so. Expat life can develop mean streaks, selfish streaks, just as much as it can empower altruism and other-acceptance.

- Whether willingly or not, a family's intimate experience of expat living widens their expectations of life beyond the local. The extended family see that you can live another way. If you as an expat are the first of your family, or the only one in your family, to successfully live abroad, your journey is seen as amazing, exceptional, and so it is. But for those following, this is now just another option. And one you have given people permission to emulate; if you can do it so can they. They just have to follow what you did.

As parents, we have consciously worked with our children since we moved and left them in university to build success together, apart. Our lives have been enhanced beyond belief by our commitment to each other. We still have the odd parenting bit to do; often they will parent us

> Handled sensitively, and provided relationships are recognised as two-way streets and worked on accordingly, the benefits of expat living on the whole family can outweigh the struggles by a long margin.

now. We are firm friends, with the added respect and acceptance for our unconventional and growing roles in each other's life. We annoy each other. We avoid too much interference in each other's life. We support each other's professional and personal development. We enjoy each other's company. We look forward to visits and shared holidays. We are immensely proud of each other. And we love the extended family. Our daughter-in-law and our son-in law are two of the most caring, loving individuals we have been fortunate to meet; our grandchildren brimming with life and potential. We work stuff out with one or other of them every month. They fill our lives with love and joy and wonder. We all are more because we left. Did we have wobbly times? Yes! Both financially and emotionally. Was it worth it? Absolutely!

NON-ACCOMPANYING CHILD MATTERS
BOARDING SCHOOLS

There are many excellent boarding schools worldwide that cater for all ages but it is becoming more unusual to find such facilities for the under 7s. Boarding schools exist because there is a need for them. Children are sent to board for a variety of reasons:

- Continuity of schooling environment while parents work in a variety of locations.
- Curriculum, country specific
- Curriculum opportunities for gifted learners and those with support needs
- Curriculum extras, e.g. sports, music, art, drama . . .
- Additional language learning
- Networking friendships
- Discipline
- Ease of transfer to High School and University.

Some children grow up with the expectation that they will board; for others it comes as a shock that they will be apart from their parents. Sometimes it will come as a shock to parents that their children want to board. They are the ones feeling abandoned! Life changes are challenging on so many levels. Family matters are as close to the bone as it gets. Again, there is no right or wrong choice, only best fit for all. Once you know you will be leaving, you have a number of choices to consider:

- Go alone, and one partner stays to look after the family in its current location.
- Everyone goes. Children transfer to a day school in your new location.
- Both parents go and the children board in their home country. It is likely that your company will pay the boarding fees. This can entice a family to choose this option because it is too good to pass up in terms of quality education. Weigh the non-

educational elements carefully. Not being together may be a deal-breaker.

- Both parents go and the children board in a completely different country. This may seem a strange scenario initially but in reality all boarding is a world removed from home regardless if it is 50km down the road or 1000km away in another country. Children are corralled and managed in all cases so why not in another country altogether? You may have a country specific curriculum you wish your child to enter and progress through to university. You may have family near the new boarding school. It is likely your company will pay school fees.

- Everyone goes and your children board in your new country. They are with you but not living with you. There may be travel issues that militate against a day school option in your new post. This way you get to see your children more often, and they get to experience the same new culture as you do. Again, it is likely your company will pay school fees.

Note on school fees:

Boarding school fees are expensive. You are buying around the clock care for your child plus a more extensive curriculum opportunity than a day school. There are four main ways to cover this expense:

1. Your company pays all boarding fees and an annual travel ticket for your child to join you during the major holiday. Health cover is included.
2. You pay all costs.
3. Your child enters boarding school on an academic, music or sports scholarship. These can be partial scholarships or full scholarships.

4. A mixture of the above. It is not unusual for a company to pay 100% fees for the first child and a reducing percentage for additional children.

5. You Home School your child.

Please beware that the actual boarding fee is only a fraction of the true cost. You will need to budget for the extras that include:

- Music tuition and exams
- Musical instruments
- Uniform – and there are many combinations to be considered, often only available from a designated uniform shop. Designated uniform providers are more expensive. The good news is – the quality is excellent. You do get what you pay for.
- School trips.
- Travel – theirs and yours
- Pocket money
- Casual clothes
- External courses, e.g. driving lessons, LAMDA, scuba diving, rock climbing . . .
- Normal family expenditure, e.g., dentist, orthodontic treatment, spectacles, contact lenses, laptop . . .
- Other, hidden stuff, like the Yearbook, etc.

Boarding schools provide an extensive service to families but you will need to do your homework to find the right fit for your child. Knowing your child's strengths and interests is a good starting point. Plan forward where you want them to be ideally, leaving room for surprising opportunity, then make a list of prospective schools that meet your criteria and visit them all. Bring your child or children with you. Their impressions count. After all, they will be the ones in situ for the majority of the year.

What should you take note of:

- Academic achievement. This record will be available on the school's website.

- First impressions: security, buildings in good shape, well maintained gardens and playing fields, cleanliness, general order, happy pupils, a good buzz about the place, professional and friendly staff, welcoming and professional head, well-structured classrooms, modern resources, purposeful activity going on, clean kitchen, well kept dormitories or bedrooms.
- Digging deeper: child focused learning, depth and breadth of curriculum, areas of interest to your child, good parent-school relationships
- Afterwards: best fit eliminations. If none meet your requirements, go back to the drawing board and add more schools to your list. Remember, you are looking for the best for your child. You may well be surprised where you find this. Do not be seduced into believing that the most expensive schools are the only way forward. Sometimes these can be ponsy and cold to an outsider – but more importantly, not the best environment for your child to flourish in.

Separating from your non-adult children is emotionally wrenching. As parents, we are generally programmed to expect this to take a similar path to our own upbringing. For many, this expectation will be that children leave home to go to university, training college or take up paid employment in their late teens. The home base remains, with parents living there.

I remember driving away from Stoneyhurst College in tears. We had just deposited our 17 year old daughter, Fionnuala, and 15 year old son, Brendan, for the new autumn term. We were immensely proud of them. They were there on academic and musical scholarships: how could we deny them the opportunity? Leaving them standing together outside the front door was wrenching but at least they were together. And we were together. And we lived 6 hours down the motorway. But that distance might as well have been to the moon! The main point was – we were going home without them. 10 km down the road we pulled onto the hard shoulder and had a good cry before continuing our long, lonely journey home.

Brendan writes:

For those of you who have never experienced a boarding school environment, or are considering one for your children, you should take a look at the Harry Potter films which do, minus the magic and 'end-of-the-world' theme, mirror what goes on a boarding school surprisingly well. I, too, took the train at the beginning and end of every school year, was also put into a House (Weld, not Griffindor), did all sorts of weird and wonderful activities, and made plenty of friends (and enemies), many of them life-long. When you take parents out the equation (except for a few minor necessities like funds, food, clothing, love, respect etc), then kids tend to create their own little worlds and just get on with the business of growing up.

There are plenty of positives about attending a boarding school. Firstly, you are given all sorts of wonderful opportunities. In a 'live-in' boarding environment, kids spend every waking hour in a learning environment, and the good schools out there lay on plenty of activities to fill those hours. These vary greatly, depending on what the child is good at. I was an all-rounder, so I got stuck into many things, such as: learning a musical instrument and playing in school orchestras and concert bands; acting on stage, whether musicals or traditional theatre; sports and physical activities, I played a lot of rugby (which in itself teaches a young man a lot about growing up); I also took up debating, a skill I believed would be useful in later life. I had plenty of friends who didn't take advantage of these opportunities, and they turned out fine as well, however if you are motivated enough (by yourself or by your parents), there is really no limit to what you can learn.

Secondly, the friends you make at boarding school are truly friends for life. The first night away from home is always the most difficult, and there are always a few tears when parents drop their kids at the door aged 6 or 12. After that initial shock, kids turn to their peers for encouragement and acceptance, and this is what makes those school-year bonds so strong and lasting. I remember feeling that I would do anything for my 'brothers', and still to this day, I feel most strongly about those friends I made in boarding school. Fast forward 10 years, and you can see how these friendships and connections can help you out in later life when you're 'looking to break into the city' or 'need a real friend'.

Thirdly, there was a strong sense of 'achievement' at boarding school, meaning that we as a peer group, and class, and school, engineered certain achievements that I as a boy then, and as a man now, still consider to be something to be proud of. One such memory sticks out. I was part of a particularly good rugby team, and in my second-to-final year, we managed to win the national rugby 7's championship. That is a moment that I will never forget, but more importantly, that taught me that with perseverance, hard-work, commitment, and the strength of friendship, you can achieve anything. These achievements sent me into the world a very rounded and confident young man, able to stand eye to eye with anyone and even when times got tough, I could look back and learn new lessons from that which I achieved at boarding school.

What about the negatives? Boarding school is not for everyone. I was lucky enough to be physically fit, musically gifted and popular with friends. I saw plenty of people for whom the boarding school environment was not a fertile paradise, rather a barren, thirsty ordeal. Most people will find a group of friends with whom they can be themselves, however for those kids with confidence issues, or behavioural problems, sending the kid away to 'straighten him out' or because 'it's more convenient' will only exacerbate the situation. I remember two or three examples of kids who started out shy and gradually drew further and further inside. I don't know how they turned out; honestly, I have difficulty remembering their names. That is not what boarding school is about.

G T Donnellan   143

The biggest negative as I see it, is the loss of intimacy with your parents. At the time, I never realised this, of course, though looking back it's as clear as day, and must have been for my parents, too. I was so busy growing up to be my own man, I often neglected to spend valuable time with my parents. I have a perfect story to illustrate this. By the time I was 17 / 18, I was 6' tall, athletic, and with a twinkle in my eye that said 'the world is my oyster'. When returning home from boarding school for the holidays, I didn't want to call my parents 'mum and dad', that was too childish. Nor did I want to call them by their first names, that was too formal. I ended up making up nicknames for my parents, 'Boris and Betty', as a sort of 'middle-ground' that told the world 'I am my own man and am making my way in the world'. It was an elegant, solution, so I thought. I never asked my parents what they thought of this. To this day, I still call them 'Boris and Betty'.

Any regrets? Sometimes I feel that I missed out on being closer with my parents, though I strongly believe that they are proud of who I have become. When my parents moved to Japan, I wonder how life would have turned out had I followed them and studied in one of the excellent universities there. However, I am old enough to know that life is the sum of the sum of the journeys you have made, not the ones you could have made. I never regret the things I achieved, the friends I made, or the opportunities I was given, and I thank my parents for giving me such a chance.

I never knew they used to cry when they left me at school. As a father myself now, I can see that parenthood is a double edged sword; you will always do the best for your children, even if sometimes it cuts deep.

UNIVERSITIES

University is an exciting time for your young adult daughter or son. It may be the first time they leave home or it may be another step along the road of their education as expat children. What tends to be measured first on this journey is the quality of provision the university or further education college brings to the dreams and hopes of the student. Another good match is important here. Your child's secondary or high school will have provided career counselling but please do not leave it all up to them. Do research with your youngster. Listen to his or her dreams. In this modern world, a first degree may lead to a complete turnaround as your adult child gets to know himself or herself better. Or your youngster may know exactly what he or she wants and there is no subsequent deviation or wobbles along the route. Either way, it is their life and they need to be assured of your support and advice along the way. The family pattern is now changing; they are getting to make the choices for themselves.

If they are leaving home for the first time, or even for boarding school, they may have a lot to learn about:

- Relationships
- Financial management
- Time management
- Looking after themselves

Relationships are tricky, none more so than the early romantic ones. An inordinate amount of self-image can be caught up in sexual exploration and gender questioning. Make sure your young adult knows about safe sexual practices and how to avoid, and deal with, sexually transmitted diseases. Miscarriages and abortions, should they occur, need to be handled with care and support, for both partners. Keep the channels of communication open. Abusive behaviour in relationships does occur; imagine this time as a training ground where practices from many different walks of life merge and mingle. To a youngster from a sheltered background, some of this activity may appeal as erotic and adventurous; to a youngster from a permissive background, this is an opportunity to get even more kinky. All you may be able to do at this stage is support the person not the behaviour. Your wonderful son or daughter is in there but they are temporarily held hostage by their own raging hormone persona.

Financial management is a hit and miss affair, sometimes for years. It all depends on how much training in money matters you have provided in the past. At any rate, it is likely your youngster will hit you for money at inconvenient times so be prepared. They will perceive all their needs as genuine whether it is beer money, rent or fashion. Depending on their chosen course, they may be able to do part time work to support their wants while you provide for their needs. Or their course is so full time there are not enough hours in the day and you cover everything! As expat parents, often times the money you are earning is not indicative of reality; it is not sustainable in the long term. Your youngster may not appreciate this and a difficulty arises when you are not able to sustain him or her in the fashion they have become accustomed to. And this continues to be an issue when he or she starts work and they have difficulty adjusting to a lower salary and standard of living.

Time management is a glorious and painful series of lessons time and again for youngsters all over the world. Unless a university course is completely prescriptive, they will have to self-manage to succeed. This is a time when it is better if your youngster lives away from home, even if it is a few doors away. It gives them the autonomy to slob it, sleep in late, miss lectures, and generally be lazy without your knowing and pulling your hair out! This is their time to learn from their mistakes and to recognise what really excites them about their chosen career path.

Learning to look after themselves is an art form that needs to be learned too because they may have been completely taken care of, and monitored, at home. The cause and effect of their actions is a good learning tool but sometimes it takes a while for the lesson to kick in.

Some youngsters will develop destructive habits because they have the freedom to experiment; others will experiment more judiciously, but experiment they will with personal freedoms, course requirements, and financial obligations. Expect weight gain, weight loss, drug use, sexual experimentation, smoking, blue hair, green hair, no hair, body piercing, tattoos, anything really that smacks of rebelliousness. The outcome of all this will determine lifelong character and successful habits.

What can you do as an expat parent? Be there for your young adult. Keep the communication door open. Accept them as they struggle to define who they are apart from the family identity. Love the person inside even as you struggle with behaviour and actions. This is their life, their choice now.

What can you do as an expat university student? Be the best you can be. Make the most of every opportunity. Keep safe, and keep others safe. Keep communications open with your expat parents. They miss you as well. A hug and a thank you go a long way.

IN WORK

There are more and more expats travelling to work when their children have grown up and are self-sustaining. This is sometimes an opportunity to:

- Experience living abroad
- Shore up the retirement fund
- Give back to society through service

If you are lucky enough to have a good relationship with your adult children, you will miss them and they will miss you. There may be some pressure on you to remain and be there for the grandchildren or some derogatory pressure regarding working abroad at your age. It is as if the shoe is on the other foot; your children are looking out for you now. How lovely, even if it is with a negative edge. At least you know they care! Stand firm. This is your life; your choice. There is nothing more exciting that a life full-lived. There is always more to learn, to experience, to give back. Live your dream, not your age!

12

EXTENDED FAMILY

IN THE ACTUAL act of moving abroad, the extended family are often reduced to the role of onlookers as you push ahead to get everything and everyone organised in a specific timeline. They cannot really help you logistically. You are the one who has to present physically for visa application; you are the one who has to sign off on the shipment; you are the one who has to get all the ducks in a row. It is all so exciting, and you are the only one getting to do it all while all your extended family can do is sit and watch. But they can offer emotional support and encouragement too; something they need to be able to give as much as you need to make time to receive. The more they feel side-lined, the more likely their support of you will wane and peter out just when you need it most. And, yes, they have made it all about them too like we spoke of earlier about work colleagues and bosses. While the change-choice is yours, and it is all about you, your action has imposed change on those around you, and people's responses can be unpredictable and bizarre. A family minefield can appear with everyone tip-toeing around everyone else and many non-flattering tales emerging as a consequence. Someone is bound to feel neglected; and that someone may well be you.

Parents will find your leaving upsetting; they will miss you and they will experience your loss from the moment you tell them you are leaving. They may take it personally, imposing an emotional guilt trip on you that is theirs alone. They may try to coerce you to stay or they may withdraw from you, leaving you emotionally isolated at the exact time you feel you have successfully pushed through your own limitations to create an exciting new opportunity for yourself. They may deliver all of the above leaving you completely confused. Or they may surprise you entirely by being super enthusiastic and supportive. This may be the moment they have been quietly waiting for; for you to shine like the star they always knew you were, for you to leave home

> There is a high emotional content to leaving parents behind.

and grow up. This is the best outcome ever. You get to live your dream with the help of those who mean the most to you. Or you may choose not to tell your parents you are leaving to avoid possible disapproval or sabotage. You have your deep seated reasons for going it alone. Or one parent may support you, the other not. There are as many possible outcomes in your leaving as there are individual expats. They all have one thing in common though: there is a high emotional content attached to leaving parents behind. But it is healthy to leave home and create a new life for yourself. The foundations of society depend on people doing just that at regular intervals. But expat living is in another country, with different norms and, usually a greater distance away, and this is another thing altogether. You have been raised for your home society. Leaving it behind may be seen as you discarding it casually and disrespectfully after all your parents, extended family and society in general have invested in you. They may find your action insulting; you may find theirs stifling.

Siblings are often the first in the family to know of an impending departure from the ranks as their help is requested in telling the parents. Not much thought is given to what their response or reaction might be. This is a mistake. You are equally an integral part of their life as that of your parents. They may feel:

- Excited for you
- Supportive of you
- Anxious for you
- Concerned for you
- Angry that you are leaving them to cope with the parents alone
- Your choice to leave may condemn them to stay, you got in first
- Jealous of your opportunity
- Depressed you will soon be living far away from them
- Thrilled that once you are gone they will be number one with their parents
- Relieved you are no longer a threat to them having the family's business, to name a few

Grandchildren will probably look in awe at their grandparents going to live somewhere else. If they lived close by, they will miss them a lot, and this needs to be handled sensitively. If they already lived a distance away, it may seem like nothing has changed as they continue to Skype chat or call regularly. Older grandchildren will make good use of their grandparents living abroad to explore new countries. Younger grandchildren may simply not understand what is going on. It is the age-group in between that may be traumatised by the sudden absence of close grandparents. This can generate a bereavement situation. All parties involved need to be sensitive to this. Expat grandparents should do a home visit as soon as possible to allay the grandchildren's fears. Alternatively, if feasible, these grandchildren should be taken to visit their grandparent's new country.

Grandparents can mourn a grandchild's expat choice while supporting the move completely. Depending on their health, age, mobility, and how close a relationship they have, they may or may not be able to visit him or her in their new country. They may simply never see each other again. They may indeed be saying goodbye for the last time. If you are close to your grandparents, it will be deeply distressing to say farewell for you all. Make sure they have some extra support as you physically leave, and for the foreseeable future. Keep in touch regularly. While a phone call may seem a little inconvenient in your busy exciting new life, the smile you will generate on their face will warm you all the way around the world. And do not let your new friends in your new culture determine your home family relationships. If you are fortunate to have such close and loving ties, celebrate it. Many expats are not so fortunate in their home family. Their dismissive bravado may belie their jealousy at your happiness.

Nieces and nephews: depending on how close your family is, you may or may not have a large number of people to say goodbye to. Responses or reactions to your leaving will vary. It is hard to be sensitive to every nuance and every person since you are in an unusual emotional state yourself but it is worth putting in as much effort as you can manage to make sure everyone gets an equal part of you. Your leaving is giving this group, in particular, a way forward they can emulate in the future. They will be watching you closely. As will their parents.

So what might your parents, brothers, sisters, grandchildren and grandparents, nieces and nephews think about you leaving? For some, they think so little about you leaving that you would be surprised. For others, it is all they can talk about. Some go into a silent, reproachful depression. Others are so excited to see you go that you begin to wonder! But chances are you will have heard some of these comments:

- So you're off then and leaving me behind.
- I think you're so courageous! I could never do that!
- You've been an amazing sister/uncle/granny. I'll be lost without you.
- So, you're too good for the likes of us then?
- You're so selfish! You only ever think of yourself! Who's going to help me look after our parents?
- You won't be here for the wedding then?
- Can you find me a job when you get there?
- How will you live in that place? Does it have running water or electricity? We're always here for you if you need to come home.

Behind this selection of comments lie some empowering and disempowering beliefs that feed directly into your fragile emotional state and take up residence for just the appropriate occasion in the future. Negatively, some affirm that you are selfish and proud, while the last one prompts at failure. Often these provide the last straw in fragile relationships and when you walk away it is with anger in your heart at those you leave behind rather than excitement for what lies ahead. Positively, you are affirmed as a loving sibling who is encouraged to extend personal responsibility and provision to others back home when you are successful abroad. This is a mixed bag of blessings with a large topping of guilt as you have only room to think of one at the moment, and for many weeks and months to come. None of these states make returning to visit easy. While you forget the main thrust of the dialogue and exchanges as you integrate into your new life, they return with a sour vengeance as you turn your car into the home driveway once more. And you wonder what the hell you are doing and why you just cannot break free, be yourself and keep going!

And you wonder just how long you can keep this up since the energy seems to be all one way, you to them!

The answer lies somewhere with the twins of personality and culture. We are nurtured to behave in a typical cultural way from early childhood. If you are experiencing difficulty in relationships as you move away, it may simply be because you see things differently, and one of the key components here is that you see you are free to choose how you want to live. Culturally, others may agree with you, but experience this freedom of choice only locally. Suddenly, your thinking outside the box is threatening the status quo. You never know how many people want to escape their humdrum lifestyle but feel obliged to conform for the sake of others; often others who hold an emotional chokehold on them to their detriment. When expats feel more at home with other expats rather than extended family it is because they recognise a similar way of thinking that lies outside the confines of home culture: interestingly, the expats can be from a variety of home cultures, not just have one in common. Your expectations and perceptions are now more finely tuned with that group of fellow expats; those of your home culture stand out in stark contrast. You have left for something better, and you have found it. But the extended family still calls. Our elastic ties may be stretched to breaking point but few expats completely break all ties.

You know what you want to gain in your new life but do you know what you stand to lose from leaving your home? You will miss key family points, e.g. births, deaths, steps to maturity along the way. You miss holiday celebrations together, either completely, or regularly. Children or grandchildren, nieces and nephews, grow up without you. Communication has patchy points. It may even peter out altogether. You run the risk of becoming stateless over time even though you will always be what your passport says you are. And there are a myriad of other small happenings that make a difference in family connection.

There are two major areas that are extremely difficult for an expat. Both are distance related.

1.   A parent needing to be looked after in a Nursing Home or hospital. Whilst the responses to this necessity are often dealt with calmly and logistically, emotions ride high under the surface; guilt being the major player for the offspring, anxiety for the patient. The expat may or may not be in a financial position to assist with this expense, or it may already have been provided for. But the one thing that cannot be measured, and often not provided, is time. Time to visit. Time to listen. Time to hold hands. And family in the 'home' situation take the brunt of the provision. The expat dips in annually, stirring up emotions in the patient and leaving the others to pick up the pieces when they leave. It is difficult for everyone. But the expat carries the brunt of the guilt, by choice. The 'what-if' questions run in circles inside their head alongside the 'might haves', the 'should haves', and the 'could haves'. This is a very real face of an expat's choices. It cuts deep but you may have no option but to walk away; you chose to live in another time and place but this part of your heart never really left. You feel the depth of your fractured life to the full during these moments. You question yourself if you have done the right thing. This is a real cost of expat living measuring what you are missing rather than what you are gaining.

My mother was in a nursing home for a few years before she passed away. She was wheelchair bound and needed special care that couldn't be provided at home any more. While her body degenerated her mind became all the sharper. It was difficult for her to lose control of her surroundings, and difficult for us watching it happen.

There was an additional difficulty in all of this and that was me. I was the only one of her children living away from home, far away from home. My siblings bore the brunt of looking after her every need willingly but I was out of this loop. I returned every summer and she was delighted. I can only imaging their chagrin when I was the only one she would talk of then when they were pandering to her every day! Then I would go away again and she would hit rock bottom, and they had to pick up the pieces again, and I picked up my own pieces far away in my place of work choice. Working away from home and loved ones hurt. I ask myself why I do this. Is it all worthwhile? There are days I say 'Yes' and there are days I say 'No'.

2. The death of a family member. This can unexpected or one waited unwillingly for but whatever the reason, when it happens, the effect is multiplied by the distance apart. There is a deep grieving process for the loss of the family member, and a deep grieving process for all that was lost to the expat. While you keep the pain at bay, you have effectively to get yourself half-way around the world; deal politely with people who, even in good times, yanked your chain; and step to a routine that is deeply embedded in the home culture you have long since abandoned. And step you should. This is a routine that fulfils the deepest needs of society. You can give back that much.

But what of those family members waiting to welcome you back? Are they all happy to see you again? Maybe. Maybe not. After all, your leaving caused an imbalance in the family. You stirred things up. Now they have to put up with you landing in amongst them to take your rightful place again. Sometimes, the best that can be said and done is to behave dispassionately and maturely.

There is one other point that begs to be returned to here: it is the grieving process. It continues along a different route for the expat. When you go 'home' for a family member's funeral, you experience the searing emotions everyone else is experiencing, perhaps a little ameliorated by jetlag. Then you leave, and the leaving and the distance provide a dulling barrier, and when work takes over again, the time to grieve is cut short. It does not belong in your new life canvas. But when you return 'home' again, and stand in that cemetery, it is as if the intervening months and years melt away and you are returned with a deep ferocity into the grieving process of the actual moment. Local family accompanying you may be completely dumbfounded at the outpouring of your grief; they have moved on but you have not had that time, in that particular location, to do so. I wondered as a child, when cousins would visit from the UK or America, why they would be so upset when they visited the cemetery. It was to be many years later when I returned to my sister's grave from China, months after her funeral, that I experienced first-hand what they did. Distance only interrupts the grieving process.

My Mum died when I was in Tokyo. I got the call to come home early in the morning; the one we all dread, the ringing of the phone that rouses you from sleep instantly. My husband had just gone away on business to Brunei and I was all alone, half a world away from where my Mum lay dying. I called him, interrupting his sleep, and then packed for leaving. Then I had to wait. Wait for the airline offices to open to buy an emergency ticket; wait for my school to open so I could arrange time off; wait for daylight until I could phone my children in America and Czech Republic. All I could do was frantically wait while my Mum drifted away from me. As day broke I couldn't wait anymore; I took a taxi to the airport and waited for the airline desks to open. I was fortunate. I got home in time to talk to her once more; to hold her hand as she lay sleeping; to kiss her forehead in the presence of my siblings just after she slipped away.

It was a painful time for all of us. I had my regrets to deal with; to hold those in contrast to my choices that had taken me away for most of my life. I had my jealousies to deal with; my siblings had more time with her than I did. I had my siblings to deal with; to second guess; to follow; to love; to annoy; to escape from, and to run to. I remembered the good times with my mother; I remembered times best forgotten. And I wondered what would happen all of us. Whether we would stick together or retreat to lick our wounds. Was our family gone now? You see, she had held us all together. She was our focus whether we lived beside her or half way around the world.

Could we now evolve to be other focussed? Or was this truly the end of an era?

As in so many cases there were elements of all of this in the following years. We retreated and dispersed for a while but gradually found a way back again that we own ourselves now. And she is there in the smiles of our grandchildren, in their dark brown eyes or curly hair. And my grieving lessened with each visit.

EXTENDED FAMILY MATTERS

Culture and personality are key determinants in life choices. Personal expectations and preconceptions light the way forward. Extended family is a cocoon or a springboard; very occasionally, it is both.

Note 1: there are certain commonalities that every expat experiences when returning home to visit. I delve into this in more depth in **Expat Life: Carousel Moves.** For the moment let me mention three things here briefly:

1.   Those expats that return to visit regularly or irregularly for a variety of reasons do so out of a sense of love, familial duty, and /or genuine friendship. Some are searching for acceptance; some closure. For all, this is a conscious decision although regularly they are aware they will face some type of negative grief. It is never a holiday but it may be all the holiday the expat will experience that year or those years. It is often sacrificial: this time home takes all their savings. Some goes into personal preparation; after all, one has to put one's best face forward: some will be gobbled up by travel costs; some will be given in gifts or family needs provision.

2.   Expats change during their time abroad. They are not the same person that left. Sure, that person still remains but they have added a new culture. Culture experience is additive and subtractive; you gain new elements of one at the loss of elements of the other. You literally see the world differently. You are not being poncy. Extended family back home change over time too but this change is relative to your home culture so it can be difficult to see what has actually changed except from physical mobility or the ageing process. Maybe your niece is driving now; maybe she had a steady boyfriend. Your family back home cannot see the world as you see it. But you can see the world as they see it. A disconnect exists. You will likely experience this most forcefully in conversations about your new life. You will be excitedly recalling some experience and, as you watch, their eyes glaze over during the telling and before you can finish they interrupt with some

inane comment, for you, but excruciatingly real for them, about a neighbour's demise. The truth is, you can move towards them but they cannot move with you anymore. Despite your frustration, your anger, the ball is firmly in your court. You will need to find a way to celebrate your growth while supporting theirs – in their world. They may, in the end, be completely disinterested in your life abroad and you may have to decide how sustainable this one-sided relationship is. Additionally, they may be insanely jealous about your good fortune and you get only one side of the story when you are visiting. The rest goes around about by word of mouth and eventually it will get back to you what they really think about you and your new life. If you have experienced this, remember it reflects on them not on you. What they think about you is something you cannot change, only manage.

3.   Home family members will be excited about you visiting. They too will spend money preparing for you. This may be their way of acknowledging how much further away you have moved; how much more you command in nice surroundings, etc. Every little improvement they do is a jewel in their year, something they will enjoy after you leave, and which will be imbued with a sense of you – 'we got that for when Brendan came home'. They will be acutely aware that you have moved on. They will be anxious about being able to touch base with you again. Sometimes when they overshare about local events, it is to dispel the initial awkwardness they are experiencing as well as a desire to get you as up to date as possible as quickly as possible so you will know what is going on; whom to congratulate; whom to sympathise with. You may not be in the least interested. Is it any surprise then that they may not be interested in your story? Share in short bites with a minimum of pictures. An overshare from you will indicate how uninteresting their life is in your eyes. And don't forget to record your time together. While they may resist photographs they will be chuffed to know you will carry their pictures back to your new home. At least, they can be present with you in this way.

Becky writes:

The plane touches down at Incheon airport, and I breathe a sigh of relief. I swear to myself that I will never try to cheat the airline industry again by taking a long layover. After being kicked out of the tiny airport in Shenyang twice (once when the departures hall closed, once when arrivals closed) and being shuttled out to a small nearby hotel, if you want to call it that, by a good Samaritan and paying $80 for a room of questionable character, I have learned my lesson. Just pay the damn money and get a direct flight.

It's the first time I've been back to Korea in two years, yet it feels like getting back into my own skin. If I could relive the previous night at a small town in Korea, it would be a lot less harrowing. I would get a taxi, ask for a jjimjjilbang (bath house) or PCbang (internet café) or any of a number of other businesses that are typically 24 hours and are sprinkled liberally around just about any neighbourhood in most towns and definitely any place big enough to have an airport. I wouldn't even have to take a taxi; in Korea, I often walked alone after one in the morning, and could wander my way around until I found what I needed. I often consider Korea my second home; when I came to Shanghai, I settled in a heavily Korean neighbourhood. I love Korea, and Korea loves me. Sarang-hamnida!

Now, if you'd told me, seven years ago when I first came to Korea to teach English, that I would ever feel this way about this country, I would have laughed in your face. My first month was excruciating. I was terrified of my boss. In my orientation, he had explained that the mothers of our students were wealthy, powerful, and, since they didn't work, they had both the time and the means to ruin my life if I upset them. He followed it up by promising that if I did my damn job and kept everyone happy, we'd be cool, but that if not, he'd f**k me up.

(Please note: my boss may have been Korean ethnically, but culturally he was 100% New Yorker).

Three weeks later, I'd managed to piss off one of these wealthy, powerful women. Her son was less mature than the other kids in the class, and his behaviour was an issue. I'd mentioned it in the parent journal we sent home every day, and on the day in question I elaborated, at her request. There was another behaviour incident that day, and I took him out into the hall to talk about it with one of the Korean staff members.

Like any mother, hearing something negative about her child put her on the defensive. Then her son, we'll call him little Timmy, got upset, and told her one of the girls, Suzie, let's say, was mean to him that day. Well, Timmy's mom and Suzie's mom have each other on speed dial, so the former calls the latter and finds out that I didn't write anything about Suzie being mean to Timmy. And since she was already on the defensive, Timmy's mom jumps to the conclusion that I am being unfair.

And that was before Timmy's dad came home and heard his son say I'd hit him.

Well, it seemed a little creepy when I first found out there were cameras all over the school, but I'll tell you, never in my life have I been so grateful for video surveillance. The boss brought her in and showed her the incident from beginning to end to demonstrate that I wasn't a child-eating monster without making her lose face. She sent little Timmy to a different school two months later, but honestly, I was relieved more than anything. I survived the first month, but never totally lost my discomfort around class parents.

In addition to a scary boss and over involved, powerful mothers, I had language and food to contend with. The English saturation around Seoul is pretty high, but I couldn't read Korean, and even the adopted English words were often adapted to Korean pronunciation, an amalgamation known as Konglish. Get in a cab and say you want to go to Samsung Plaza, and you'll get a blank look. Tell them "Som-sung Puh-la-juh" and you'll get a cheerful, "O-Kay!" The food was nearly as incomprehensible as the language. In fact, it was so intimidating, with its thousand side dishes and strange ingredients, that I'd been there three months before darkening the doorway of a Korean restaurant. (Luckily there was a McDonald's not too far from the school, and the aforementioned Samsung Plaza had several Italian restaurants. Let me tell you, Italian cuisine is really hard to screw up, although personally I don't care to eat it with sweet pickles). Friends probably would have helped with the adjustment, but I didn't really hit it off with any of my colleagues.

In short, I really struggled. My saving grace was my church. Say what you will about us Mormons and our strange beliefs, but we are everywhere, and we believe those same strange beliefs no matter where you go, and they include helping one another out. This was a factor in my decision-making process when I chose to take a calculated risk and come to Korea – a place well-known for screwing over dopey English teachers – completely alone. I knew there were branches of the Church of Jesus Christ of Latter-Day Saints in Seoul, even a temple, and if I had the church, somehow I'd be okay.

But the church just helped me to survive. My faith was pretty strong, but it didn't transform Korea into the magical wonderland I regard it as now. It took friends to do that. That first time I went into a Korean restaurant, it was with friends (friends I made at church, so the argument could be made that my faith gave me more than just survival, but we'll make them separate issues for arguments' sake). It was a friend from church who invited me to go to a Korean bath house for the first time. It should have seemed strange, someone asking me if I wanted to join a group of friends to go get naked together and bathe, but I figured when in Rome, do as the Romans do...especially when it's a Roman of your faith inviting you to get all Roman. And for the record (for those of you coming from a similarly puritanical background as me), five minutes into the experience, nobody really cares that you're naked anymore. Seriously. It was these same friends who taught me to grill my kimchi (a technique which works wonders on a food all of us wei-guk must "acquire a taste for"), took me to my first noraebang (private karaoke room), my first DVDbang (private theater room), and my first board game café.

It was these friends that showed me I wasn't alone in my struggles. They helped me to laugh at the ridiculous moments when they happened. They cried along with me when the homesickness got bad, and celebrated with me when I spent my first Christmas away from my family. Without them, I would have been lost.

All my time in Korea, I lived and worked in a suburb of Seoul called Bundang – sometimes known as a "bedroom city" because it is close enough for people to commute to jobs in the capital. This was a little problematic because all these church friends lived scattered around greater Seoul, so it got pretty lonely during the work week. But on the upside, it was sometimes nice to have separation. It is really easy to fall into a sort of incestuous relationship with your colleagues when you're an English teacher. You get to this new country, and your co-workers become your readymade friends. You go drinking together. You go clubbing together. You go on holidays together. You probably even live in the same neighbourhood and possibly even the same building. And when shit hits the fan, you can't escape those people, because you work with them, too. And it's in the nature of friends for shit to hit the fan from time to time, but you give each other some space, and eventually you cool off and come around. But when you can't have space because you are ALWAYS together, things just get awkward. I saw it happen a lot with my fellow teachers.

It's strange, because these friends are often the products of necessity. You need friends. I learned this on my expat journey in Bahrain – it wasn't the culture, the bad school, the bad students, or the climate that did me in; it was the failure to build a solid friendship with someone I could rely on. So we make friends where we find them. Maybe you'd be friends with these people if you knew *them at home – probably you wouldn't. If you're lucky, the day you go your separate ways is the point when you learn which it is.*

But sometimes you learn while you're still in the thick of things, and on the other hand, sometimes when that happens having distance doesn't help. I had a falling-out with some of my church friends about seven months into my contract. We hardly ever saw each other as a result, and I guess we just decided we were friends for a "season," if you subscribe to the reason/season/lifetime theory of relationships. This was a turning point for me in Korea; it marked the time where my life went from being compartmentalized between workweek and weekend to fluid. I'd like to take credit for taking my fate into my own hands, but really I just got lucky. A fresh influx of teachers had come into my school, and they changed the whole workplace dynamic. I had a new best friend, a fellow Missouri girl who helped to bridge the gap between me and some of the old blood. I'd gradually gotten over the fear of my boss, and immersed in the school's social life, I learned that he was a pretty cool guy. I worked up the nerve to ask my direct supervisor if she knew where I could learn some Korean cooking, and she offered to teach me herself. I taught myself to read the Korean alphabet, and made friends with some of the Korean teachers, too.

In short, I'd started to Live. Now I was the one taking people to the bathhouse, introducing them to the underground shopping arcade at the express bus terminal, and teaching which buses got you into the area of Seoul they wanted the fastest. And you know what? I was damn good at it. I became a bit of a walking encyclopedia. My friends would call me up to ask for directions and I could guide them, giving visual landmarks and often the number of intersections they needed to pass through. I knew where you could get everything from imported brownie mix to Burt's Bees lip balm. I knew where you could find an internet café in most of the high-traffic areas of Seoul (I didn't own a computer for most of my time there). I could tell you where to go for burritos, gyros, curries, or kebabs.

Korean phrases worked their way into my vocabulary. Not just taxi and restaurant words, either. Someone would tell me a juicy bit of gossip and I ask, "Chin-ja?" (Really?) Someone would hack me off and "Aish-shi" (the slightly less profane equivalent of shit), would slip out. Or my boss would tease me and I'd glare at him and say, "Chug-go-llae?" (His normal response was that when I asked if he wanted to die with that inflection it sounded dirty rather than like a threat, so my pronunciation still needed some work.)

And I haven't even mentioned K-Pop yet! Some of the cheesiest music on the planet, and it still never fails to bring a smile to my face. Korean MTV was a big hit in our apartment, when we weren't watching reruns of Sex in the City (without the commercials – the Korean stations air 20 minutes of commercials at the beginnings of shows, a tactic I approve of. Most nights we watched them anyways – Daniel Henney was our favourite half-Korean model and he was in a lot of commercials back then).

Sixteen months after coming to Korea, I found myself saying, "Annyeongi-keseyo." I had extended my contract, going home in time for Christmas with plenty of time to prepare for the big international teaching fair at the University of Northern Iowa in early February. This meant that my last day of teaching was our Christmas performance. It was a gut-wrenching day. I was putting on a show, then saying goodbye. Koreans truly value their teachers, and I got a lot of gifts that day. The hardest student to tell goodbye was one I'd been teaching for the whole of my time there, the one that little Timmy's mother thought I was favouring, all those months ago. When I became her teacher, she was famous for her temper tantrums, but since then she'd grown up a lot. She had difficulty with the fact that I was leaving, and kept erasing the day from our classroom calendar. But that day she told me she understood. A few days before, I told her I'd take her to America with me, that I'd pack her in my suitcase and I'd take her home. She was concerned because her family would miss her. I told her that my family missed me, too. The card she gave me with her gift – a designer scarf – said that she didn't want me to go but it was okay because my father missed me.

That night, my friends sent me off with Korean barbecue and karaoke. It was a longstanding tradition, and it kept me from getting too emotional, too early. My direct supervisor was going to the airport with me the next morning, as she was also flying home for Christmas. Several of the teachers went back to her apartment, but I went for one last bath, and cried silent tears into my bathwater. I wasn't ready to leave yet. In such a short time, Korea had become my world, and yet, I was leaving. I shivered my way back to the apartment, and spent the night packing up the last of my stuff before leaving for the airport. Having my supervisor-cum-cooking teacher share that final bus trip with me meant the world. I came to Korea alone, but somehow I lacked the courage to leave the same way.

Somehow I made it home. Somehow I got used to being able to ask for what I wanted instead of having to act it out. Somehow I adjusted to driving again instead of taking two buses and a subway (that probably sounds like an easy adjustment, but I'd gotten used to having all that reading time). Back in the states, my cool Korean phrases got vacant stares of incomprehension. I was lucky, because my friends were all Mormon, and because we send missionaries just about everywhere, they'd either been on a mission or had family who had and felt some kind of connection to the wider world. Other homecoming expats have a harder time; they are trying to tell what it was like to be on a bus on the east coast going the wrong way toward the DMZ, smelling freshly sun-dried cuttlefish because every passenger was carrying them, passing tank traps that were over 50 years old to end up at some sort of bus depot, the last passenger...only to be met with a sort of blank look and, "Er, how exciting..........Well, I've finally got our little Trinket weaned off the nipple."

Sometimes the person I'd become came as a shock. After working nearly a year and a half for a man who could use the word f**k as a noun, verb, adjective, adverb, and exclamation, I came home less of an innocent than I set out. I was sharing a changing room with my cousin and my sister's best friend as we tried on bridesmaids dresses. "Suck it in a little, and I think I can get it up," said Monica to Jenee as they worked on the zipper.

"That's what he said!" I chimed in, laughing hysterically. They laughed, then asked what the hell had happened to me while I was away.

I dutifully sent out letters of application to schools attending UNI's fair, and came home with a contract to teach K-12 art in Bahrain. I was going where I wanted to go, teaching my own subject. I just had to get through six months in America before I left. I called my best chin-gu, the Missouri girl, to tell her the exciting news, and she told me our school was still scrambling to hire teachers for March. That was terrible. That was awful. They were such a good school. It was...it was an opportunity my sister loved me enough to point out. Why shouldn't I go back to Korea in the meantime? I sent emails to my bosses, and in less than a month, found myself back on Korean soil, as if I'd never left. And to this day, that feeling hits me every time.

Maybe my life would have been easier if Korea had been a struggle from beginning to end. I hit the ground in Bahrain excited to overcome all its obstacles, just as I had in Korea. I used the phrase, "In Korea," a lot those first few months; in fact, I think that was something that annoyed the hell out of one of my roommates from the start. I kept feeling slapped in the face when I realized the obstacles were completely different, and that some of them didn't get any better. Some got worse – I fell into the work-friends trap here, and had a very awkward second half of the year when my roommates and I stopped getting along around Christmas. And we didn't get a fresh batch of teachers in mid-year to save me. I kept thinking, "It wasn't like this in Korea," and on the frustrated days that became, "Why did I ever leave Korea?" and one day that question became, "Why don't I go back?"

Of course, when I actually seriously started thinking about leaving, that wasn't really the plan. I knew from a career perspective I needed to stick with art education. I put in applications and got a couple of job offers, but would have been working at schools in China and getting paid less than I could afford to. It was late in the year, and in the end, the comfort and predictability of Korea was too tempting. The truth is, I might be there still, if it weren't for the fact that in that last year everything changed. My direct supervisor moved to Greece and got married. One of our vice-principals had a baby and quit. They replaced her with someone nobody liked, who was incompetent to boot. And even my scary boss, in the end, threw in the towel, after working for the school for almost ten years. Go back? There was nothing to go back to. This year, when I started applying for new jobs, I was initially excited about the vacancy at one of Korea's best international schools, Seoul Foreign School. But I think it would just be too different. I wouldn't be living in Bundang. I wouldn't be teaching my little class of ten ankle biters. I wouldn't have a scary Korean boss come storming into the staffroom to cuss like a virtuoso. It wouldn't be the same.

I still love Korea, I still look forward to vacations there, I still compare life here to life there, whether I'm in China or the Emirates, and I imagine I still will when I move to Mongolia in August. But I hear other adventures calling me out.

13

JOB MATTERS

THERE ARE SIX things that speak directly to job matters particularly, and life in general, wherever you are in the world: qualifications, core beliefs, personal values, perceptual viewpoints, personality, and gender. But in an expat context, these take on a decidedly more critical nuance. There is usually a defined timeframe in place from the outset. And if the job does not work out for you and for your employers, you will have to leave the country, and you may have nowhere to go at short notice. You have moved into a dependency situation with the job contract.

QUALIFICATIONS are the academic, professional, and experiential elements you need to perform the job you are hired to do. Qualifications matter in an expat move. What other countries are looking for in expat hire is the additional element that is not currently available in their country. This is usually, but not exclusively, of a professional nature. Job openings do exist for the manual labourer but in some countries these are not open to expats; or conversely, only open to expats from specific designated countries, e.g. currently in

China, only Chinese nationals can work as ayis or cleaners; alternatively Japan will allow in workers from the Philippines or India to work in this capacity. Some countries do provide training programs in certain areas for expats in a desire to acquire the workforce they need, e.g. training programs in farming and manufacture in Australia at the time of going to print. Additionally, the US offers Green Cards[9] periodically to a certain demographic they wish to attract to boost their economy. Whatever your qualifications or work experience, there are opportunities in other countries for you to explore. These opportunities are additionally available to trailing spouses if they meet the necessary criteria in the country of their new move.

While your initial contribution to your expat move is your expertise, your foreign employer's contribution is your work visa. They sponsor you into their country, vouching for you, and assisting you through the legalities. This is a symbiotic relationship. They are saying to the authorities that they cannot do their business without you; you cannot work there without their compliance, all legally speaking, of course. They take the risk of you being better on paper than in reality; of you not being able to adapt to the culture, or not being even interested in doing so; of you breaking contract and leaving them in the lurch. You take the risk of working in an environment that is hostile to your attempts on improvement; that requires you to be on call 24/7; that blames the foreigner for anything that goes wrong; of becoming the shop front token foreigner while work goes on as before. The ideal, which is achieved much more often than not, is a true partnership of equal benefit to both. Will this be a hassle free nirvana? Unlikely, if true learning from each other is to happen. Perceptual positions will need to be shifted on both sides regularly. This requires a great deal of maturity on both sides but once embarked on will bring rich life-long learning and that jewel in the crown, cross-cultural enrichment.

---

[9] Green cards entitle a person to legally obtain work in the US

Our **CORE BELIEFS** develop from our personal life experiences. What we believe to be true is really true for us. They reveal themselves in our opinions about everything in life, e.g.

- Relationships
- Health
- Money
- And in this case, work

We can identify our core beliefs by observing how our opinions differ from others. We react to others whose beliefs differ from ours. We recognise in others what we ourselves believe. Do we cluster in familiar groups? Why socialise with these individuals and not those others? This is reminiscent of the old saying, 'birds of a feather flock together'. It is not a new phenomenon. But you may not recognise it as indicative of your core beliefs. Sometimes, fear and anxiety at finding yourself in a strange new environment will push you towards familiar groups you would otherwise have avoided. This is ok. Find your feet and move on when you are ready.

In your work day, whom do you identify with more? Who shares the same opinions as you? Are your conversations uplifting or critical? Along which path do you encourage each other? Are there people you avoid? Why? There is no right or wrong core belief, only ones that serve us well, or not. When you find a core belief being challenged the first thing you will notice is your sense of disbelief. Deeper challenges are identified by your sense of outrage. Let these indicators serve you well. Recognise what is going on and if you have need to review and moderate your core beliefs, do so.

In an expat journey, the following opposite pairs are commonplace to observe:

- This is a vibrant city, full of exciting places to explore.
- This is very foreign. I can easily get lost here.

- There is a real desire for improvement.

- The workers are going to be so resistant to working differently.

- Well, they didn't tell me that at interview!
- That's an interesting twist!

- The language is impossible to learn!
- Blocking off language learning times is a beneficial use of my managerial time.

The exciting thing about the above representative opinion pairs is that what we believe to be true WILL manifest as true in our experience. Our fears and negativity resolve into our 'new' world as ordinarily as our hopes and joy. The good news is that we get to choose which core beliefs are helpful to hold on to. And, we can change what we believe. Better to make a positive change and live with egg on our face than continue with a set of core beliefs that are tearing us down just to remain in the comfort group. For example, is it helpful to continue to believe that your boss will not promote you if you do not go out drinking with him every Friday after work? This may indeed be true culturally but does it extend to expats? Promotion in some cultures is offered on seniority and being one of the boys; among expats, the best person for the job usually gets it. If you have always gone out with the boss from a belief point of not doing so would mean non-promotion, and you find this is not true, changing that belief will free you to make different plans on a Friday night or continuing as before but from a different rationale.

Note: if you habitually undertake some action that is niggling you, or it is just not sitting quite right with you, look at what you believe to be true around the situation. Chances are your core values are being challenged.

A subjective bottom line here is: if you do not like a country before you go there, do not go at all if you are not prepared to change. The onus is on you to change. If not, your experience will be negative from the start. And all around you will be affected by your negativity. And your pre-departure beliefs will be validated by your ever-increasing isolation in your new country as people escape your company.

Living, and working, as an expat is challenging but it is positively life-changing. The very process of living among different races promotes a deeper understanding of the world than any Nat Geo program can provide. Ultimately it is about living and working with people whose core beliefs are formed differently than our own. So what? This is what you have come to experience and learn from. The challenge is to see through someone else's eyes. There are more similarities than differences.

Sue shares her first impressions of China:

Going to China knowing little to nothing about it was my best decision, I never had a desire to go to Asia, the job fell in my lap as most good things in my life have. I was a stranger in a strange land or lands as it would turn out.

The whistle blows and the quiet is quickly destroyed, doors slamming and shuffling feet. Still uncomfortable from the 'western style' rice-stuffed omelette forced upon me the night before by a kindly school rep, I walk in a stiff jet-lagged haze out my balcony-kitchen combo to the window and gaze out at what seems to be thousands of indistinguishable students in a similar haze pouring out of doors like lava. Maybe body-snatched zombies would be a better description for all of us. This is my new life....

SARS was just wrapping up in Canada and I managed to get it in my head that I would teach English to pay for teacher's college. The small school I was volunteering with also recruited and within two weeks I was on my way from hometown population 300,000 to the fastest-growing city in China where no one was sure how many people there actually were but the estimates were over 10 million.

The sweatshops of Factory Girls were not far away and easy to find just walking by in the street during summer.

My first adventure outside the school walls happened less than 10 minutes up the pedestrian road after making it through the guarded gate. I was hit with a wall of rain rendering my umbrella a piece of garbage and soaking me to the skin. When I arrived back at the guardhouse, Power, the security guard, looked at me sheepishly trying not to laugh. He had no way to communicate and I was too tired to really be upset but I was not ready to laugh yet either. I had survived my first monsoon.

My students were rich kids who were not up to the very competitive national standard (due to so few university spaces) and who hoped to attend university in Canada since they would not get into a Chinese university. Some of them became my friends, guides to the unknown dimensions of China in exchange for sharing the wonders of the west.

Soon after my arrival it was Teacher's Day. The school was paying for all the teachers to be bussed to a seaside resort. I couldn't wait to go swimming in the sea. All I had was a bikini and I thought nothing of whipping off my t-shirt and shorts ready to run into the ocean. Bob's wife picked up my t-shirt and insisted I put it on. I did not understand how inappropriately the Chinese people thought I was behaving. They all wore huge grandma-style bathing suits and didn't swim until dusk or even dark when no one could see them. Using the word 'swam' is generous, for the most part they just frolicked, hardly any of them knowing how to swim. The huge dinner, like an over-the-top wedding reception, was overwhelming. We had copious amounts of fish and some variety of offal. The beer was warm and since we were Westerners, lots of Coca-Cola was on offer. The Chinese principal enjoyed drinking bei zhou with us to show our solidarity. Bei zhou are like white alcohol shots that taste like paint thinner. I was a light- weight (120 lbs.), not much of a drinker. Luckily the guys covered for me when I had had enough.

Then we all got to go up on stage to sing the Canadian National anthem. Singing was a regular occurrence at staff events for 'the Canadians', a requirement of sorts.

Learning Chinese in Shenzhen is next to impossible. Every employee at my school had a different regional dialect so when I thought I had mastered a word, let alone a phrase, I was quickly corrected, each person believing their dialect was the most accurate and nationally accepted. Going to the wet market I finally figured out that the true Shenzhen locals, fishermen bought out by Zhou En Lai, spoke Cantonese. My Cantonese wet market angels accepted my pathetic Cantonese attempts with good humour, always willing to teach me more. The ladies with chapped hands and floral arm sleeves helped me understand that most Chinese people were just hoping for a laugh and a smile, unlike my career-driven Chinese co-workers.

The other ladies who fascinated me without knowing it were the cleaning ladies in straw hats with shopping bag veils to keep the sun off their necks or faces, turning like sun umbrellas as they swept the streets of Shenzhen and residing four to a storage container. While they were out sweeping with old branches during the day, I would drop off vegetables from the wet market at their door. These women were also in good humour, which I absorbed by osmosis. I now know they were probably migrant workers, working illegally, trying to make money to send home, looked down on by most and making a pittance.

It's amazing what families endure to make money. Spouses were often divided by half of China, their only child being raised by their sometimes elderly parents in their hometowns. Families that stayed together were no better off, child abuse and sexual abuse a non-issue, high school students at 18 thinking nothing of having 2 abortions. Connie was tough, a cool kid who reminded me of Rizzo from Grease. There had to be a reason. She showed up one day with a black eye. When I asked what happened she began crying. The kids with stronger English helped me understand that her father did it when he drank. I told her that my father drank too but I was lucky because he didn't hit. She cried harder, the rest of the class shocked I said it straight out like that. I held her hand and told her that when I was around my father I was turtle, keeping the soft protected under the hard because I was all I had and I had to guard myself. She could do it too until she could make her life her own. I could have said it to any of them to a certain degree; to them it was wisdom they'd never considered. As it was when I grew up, I did what I was told until I didn't. Some of the kids were spoiled, completely dependent, yet quite possibly would be sent to Canada in the next six months to a level of freedom the most mature teens would not be able to handle.

The boys hid behind their bravado. One boy from Taiwan, Romeo in the school play, was to be sent back the same day as the performance. The relations between China and Taiwan were heating up and his parents wanted him back with them. He was one of my favourites, him and his friends. They invited me to the 'goodbye' party. It was like a teen version of the mafia. Twelve 17- year-olds sitting around smoking cigarettes, drinking alcohol in a private room of a restaurant, impressed that a girl (me) could do shots and smoke cigars. When it was time to go back through the guarded gate they sent me ahead so I wouldn't get in trouble; talk about a reality check. These guys were used to the good life and I was only starting to realize how rich they were. These guys smuggled food into the school through the fence because the school food was so awful.

Saving face, the concept of pomp and circumstance, deference to those above you in the perceived hierarchy surprised me. Almost a caste system, yet I was in a 'communist' country. I am still trying to learn the nuances of this concept and I doubt it will ever be clear. I respected most the Chinese teachers, trying to make money and save as much as they could to return back to their hometowns and their families, sacrificing in ways westerners would not appreciate. They worked as hard as they could six days a week, slept on Sundays and showed very little desire for a social life.

Food was a different kind of hurdle. Most of my colleagues ate at the school simply to save money. I would take my Tupperware down to get rice as a fledgling greenie knowing the Styrofoam they used was bad for the environment. For the most part the rest of the dishes looked inedible. My western colleagues introduced me to Tesco and Pizza Hut. My new favourite that I would rarely eat at home in Canada was McDonalds. After a while, Echo, my Chinese sister, started taking me out for dinner and guiding me through the menu. I would pay for dinner and she would wolf the food down as if she'd been starved. We started a cheat sheet for me to carry in my wallet so I could go to the restaurant on my own. Initially, the wait staff would panic when they saw me alone but soon I was accepted, with hesitation.

My kitchen consisted of a microwave and a hotplate deep dish. I would cook the spaghetti noodles that would rest in the colander while I prepared the sauce. I never did use the microwave. This was also where I hung my laundry to dry and the walkway to the toilet. An outside toilet in 5-degree weather was a new kind of reality, a painful reality in the middle of the night.

The rest of my apartment was one room. A full-sized fridge, a double bed, a big TV with one English Channel. There was a large chair and a small desk. My neighbours were also teachers and had to live in the same space with several family members. I couldn't even imagine. Bob, old enough to be my father, was my favourite co-worker. He coveted my Western toilet and 'borrowed' it on occasion rather than walking 10 minutes back to his regular Western-size apartment.

Living on campus was a unique experience. I would buy groceries and was told I was 'being rich', (translation: showing off) rejecting the school food and making my own which only happened a couple of times a week. For me it was a comfort rather than an extravagance. Luckily, I worked on the sixth floor and had to do stairs several times a day. My apartment was on the fourth floor. This became my fitness routine. My jogging habit faded quickly. Running around the track became an event for the security guards who would all show up when I started my laps. I was physically bigger than any of them at my 170cm 65kgs. My shorts were too short and my chest was 'huge' (34B). Which is not to say I was perceived to be a sexual object, or maybe I was to a couple, but to most of them I was just different, misunderstood. The only people I ever saw exercise were elderly. People worked too hard and did not see a need to balance their lives with exercise. I am still curious about whether I could have won if I had raced the guards.

When you go to the store and need to buy large or extra large after being a small your whole life it can mess with your head. Shoes and bras were impossible to get. Happily, I was an hour's ride from Hong Kong where I could go to feel 'normal' on the weekend. No one openly stared at me as I walked down the road. I could get Western food beyond the fast food fare available to me in Shenzhen, though we did manage to find an Irish pub before our time was up. It was 'really' expensive and far away, an oasis in the barren Shenzhen food scene. One Chinese co-worker, Nana, invited me to her home for dinner. She was a newlywed in her first 'western-style' home. Her husband and his mom came with her to pick me up. I didn't realize until I got to their very tastefully decorated place, more like a magazine layout than homey, that Nana wanted me to teach her how to use her oven and that making dinner was up to me.

Even your hair.... My hair was long at the time and I needed a trim. Red, one of the Chinese teachers, told me she would take me to her 'groomer'. Once we arrived she helped translate what I wanted, then to my shock, she left me there. The shampoo boy 'dry washed' my hair while I was sitting in my seat, that was nice, especially the head massage! Then the stylist returned with a straight razor and started chopping. Chinese hair is thick and most women like to thin it out which I don't need. Cell phones were just starting to become popular and the stylist got a call during my haircut. The money was in my pocket, ready, I left it on his station and ran out of the salon. My hair is fine and for a long time I looked like a drowned rat until the layers started to flip up like some bizarre version of Farah Fawcett's hair.

One of my favourite pastimes on Sundays was to walk around and see what I could see. Most of the neighbourhoods were new. If I got lost I would call Echo. I would find a person who seemed nice and hand them my phone. She would establish where I was and tell me what bus to take home or that I should hop in a taxi. One day, all the Western teachers decided to go to an 'artist's village'. It was a reproduction heaven. We could have bought Picassos or Monets, anything; you name it, they had it. I was so sad. The Shenzhen Museum was another point of interest and I took some of my older students. The animals on display were not properly taxonomied, eyes were displaced, some looked as though they were moulding and they smelled. The students knew something wasn't right.... I tried to put on a brave face. "Yes, these museums are just like the rest of the world's" I said.

I've educated myself and returned to a much different consumerist, flashy, money-driven China but in a whole different sense of the word. In so many ways that was the most difficult and hug-less year of my life but it taught me so much about humanity and about myself. Now living in Shanghai, I long for the truer smaller Chinese places in China - the open-faced curiosity of the old and young, the cautious bonding with my Chinese peers.

In that year I was a student, an alien, an object of fascination, a ball of nerves, a psychologist and on my good days, I hope I was an okay teacher. I will always be grateful for that time when I decided to become a teacher for the rest of my life.

– Dedicated to Bob Sinclair

Your **PERSONAL VALUES** are what are important to you. They are a further, subjective refinement of your core beliefs. These are truly important as they define who you are, your core character; how you relate to others; and how you relate to the world. We identify them easily in a crisis: they are the points we will not move beyond; the moment of non-negotiation. They define us as a person, and are not culturally dependent. They are our inner measuring sticks; our reasons for living the way we do. Society, religion, and culture often claim them as a right but I no longer believe this. I have seen love and respect in dire circumstances, and hate and vitriol in the midst of prosperity. They are singularly, wonderfully personal. Even siblings can have dramatically different personal values.

As a child, your values were your parents' values, your community values. Young children often display their parents' values in the playground at school or in the classroom or canteen, displaying, for example, either tolerance or unacceptable intolerance in ordinary or challenging situations. It is how communities grow. Values are copied. This is the creation point of culture. New independent nations, enjoying the break from hostilities and death, will define themselves differently than that of a nation that has had autonomous independence for centuries.

Pupils in Middle and High School model their leaders. The first step into self-determination begins here. Previous, and current authorities, are questioned. Emotions boil over into teenage conflict. All with regard to what is important for the young individual. Most individuals progress through this stage to become comfortable with what they believe to be important in their own lives and go on to become valuable members of society, refining their values outwardly, from local to national, and to global, as an expat. Some never emerge from their local community values: it is their choice to promote these in situ. And there are those who are part of a global community from an early age who do not have a place they call 'home', that locale of original values. And there are some countries where expats go to work that have deeply entrenched local values. Because values are so important, there is likely to be a high emotional reaction once these are questioned or challenged; an exit ensues, or serious local consequences. Most expats will move on when their values are challenged or when staying would mean compromising on something so deeply held as to be fundamental to their character. This freedom of movement is a keystone in expat living.

Key value areas for expats revolve around relationships, health, money, and work, similar to core values. Moving away from your values on any of these areas will compromise you. You will feel the stress immediately. It is then a matter of breaking point, that point where your character becomes irreparably damaged or compromised. One example might be of holding the high moral ground in a country where 'gifting' or its more commonly known name, bribing, is endemic. Breaking your moral rule once leaves you open to manipulation. After that, it is just a matter of degree, and peace of mind. And the necessity to lie you never had to explore before! Another is to do with sex. Sexual values are still more a product of 'home' community values where aberrations in conduct are managed, often without a word, so strong is the norm. When people move away they have the opportunity to explore, and define, their sexual behaviour. Some take great license with this; others wonder, playing at the edges, but stay within their previously determined patterns of behaviour. Expats have been deported from countries for inappropriate sexual behaviour; others imprisoned. In this last example, community enhances the strength of the value. Personal values are important to the person, but additionally can be what is important to that person in that particular community. Wherever the depth of importance originates, it is personal choice that activates it. You have a choice. You can live like the Romans when in Rome, or you can decide on your own path. Initially it may seem like everyone is doing 'it', whatever that is, but given time, and a wise person will give themselves time, you will notice the exceptions.

Personal values can lead to direct cultural conflict. Examples abound every day on the News. If you are determined to export your community and personal values on the uncultured heathen, then expect resistance. It is disrespectful and ignorant to enter another's home country with the sole purpose of saving them from themselves. It is also disrespectful and ignorant to ignore the survival and safety needs of the displaced and minorities. You have rights and responsibilities as a global citizen. How easy it is to make it all about rights and be selective with responsibilities. Or maybe you are more like a global nomad, foraging where you land until the food runs out or you are suitably satiated? The challenge is to leave the people and place better for you being there; and you a better person from your time there.

> It is disrespectful and ignorant to enter another's home country with the sole purpose of saving them from themselves.

PERCEPTUAL VIEWPOINTS are your personal viewpoints seen from where you are at any point in time. They will be all about you initially, and maybe ultimately too, but in between there is a chance to develop understanding by looking at life, living, and working through someone else's eyes. Core beliefs and personal values are subjective. You will filter work, and living, in your new country through your personal experiences. You may drive people mad with your constant comparing your new situation to a previous one. You may see what is best as what is best for your previous context initially. You may even fail to see what is best on the ground; fail to see the amazing people and different ways of doing things that are sustainable for your new country. You may be seen as a know-it-all jerk and bully by your new hosts. You may be seen as a saviour who will do all this development for them. Both are dangerous, and ultimately, self-defeating positions if you wish to leave a lasting legacy behind you.

Olapeju Odeh, Nigeria, writes:

I have seen Expats come and go. Have I enjoyed working with them? Yes and No.

Yes to the ones who come with ideas to share and an open mind to learn from others. These set of Expats build relationships and add value. They observe, ask questions and blend their wealth of knowledge with what is already on the ground. They encourage, build and promote sustainable growth. When they leave, though there is a vacuum, the values they leave behind live on.

On the other hand there are Expats who come, ignoring traditions, pulling down structures and people and leaving the establishment worse than they met it. These are the ones that I cannot wait to see go.

If ever I get the opportunity to work as an Expat, I will go in with the knowledge that the local staff might be weary of my presence. Not as much as trying to run me out of town but of hoping to be accepted as equals (in cases of colleagues) or as intelligent contributors to the organisation (in cases of subordinates).

My strategy will be going in and making clear from the onset, my interest in a partnership. I will go hoping to tap into their superior knowledge of my new environment and their wealth of experience. I will also go in with all intentions of sharing my own wealth of knowledge and experience. Never forgetting this unquestionable fact; 'The purpose of my employment is not to undermine or pull down but to nurture, enrich and expose'.

Who knows, I might even develop life time friendships as some wise Expats have done before me.

There is nothing wrong with this initial 'all about me' position. It is, realistically, the only one you can take. This is you making sense of your new position with the only viewpoints you have, your current ones, which are retrospectively formed. But the wise person will quickly begin to see the disconnect, and turn their attention to the other person, the local. My father told my siblings and I time and again never to criticise anyone until we had walked a mile in their shoes. This is good advice here. Make the time to 'see' your new country or location through the eyes of the locals. What is important to them? What did they have to do, endure or give up to create what you are now working at, the very thing you have been brought in to change, and possibly over their heads at that! Every day will bring multiple occasions for reflection, for trying to see from the other person's point of view. Choose occasions which will benefit most from this process. You do not have to, nor can you sustain, a continuous multi focus on tasks at hand. But by consciously opening discussion on multiple viewpoints around key tasks you will enable the locals to learn how you see things from a non-confrontational position. Once confrontation is avoided, true understanding stands a chance.

Additionally, a third party can shed light on possible misunderstanding flashpoints. Seeking advice, and taking advice, from respected colleagues who have been on the ground longer than you can help smooth the way forward for you and your local colleagues. True trust takes a long time to establish. Be steadfast, clear, consistent, and open in your encounters. Learn how the locals are steadfast, clear, consistent, and open in their encounters. Communicate the way they understand. After all, you understand it already.

And so, we start each expat journey by internalising our expat experiences. It can make us look selfish and unbending but we are feeling the weight of the new world on our shoulders. As time passes, we adapt. Some of our perceptions change; which ones change differs for everybody. What niggles us are, thankfully, easy to spot by looking at our behaviour.

- An anger flashpoint is a sure indication that we are still looking at our foreign environment with our at-home eyes. Expletives count as anger flashpoints.

- 'I can't believe this!' 'Did you see that!' comments means we are still processing our environment, measuring it against our personal values. These are unlikely to change a whole lot. You may well have encountered a non-negotiable event.

An example I encountered in China that I just could never accept was the local's habit of spitting. Reaching for the coffee in Carrefour I could hear the man beside me clearing his throat for a good old spit! I moved my feet quickly. It landed so close I was cringing! I hoped other shoppers would not slip on it later!

- Shouting at the locals. Driving on the road was a hazardous situation in my previous location. There is a disconnect between driving rules which are rigorously tested and actual practice. The general expectation is that you drive with due cognisance and respect for your fellow traveller. The reality is local drivers driving out onto a main road without looking to see if anyone is coming, the unwritten rule being, 'it is your job not to hit me'. Once you understand this, driving begins to make sense. Shouting at the locals can be a prolonged anger episode. Beware the danger you are doing to your health here. Recognise the stress signals. Chances are anyway that the locals do not give a toss! They cannot understand what you are on about. How rude of you to shout or blow your horn at them! You are elevating your blood pressure dangerously for nothing. Ask yourself: what about the situation has changed because you shouted at it? Absolutely nothing! You are becoming too associated with this.
- 'That's not going to happen while I'm here!' This is a prophetic situation in the making. If you find yourself holding back the waters, like Moses, guess what? The minute you lower your guard, the status quo re-establishes itself. It points to a misunderstanding of the power plays that exist under the radar: take heart - these are possibly under the radar for most of the locals as well, particularly if there is a

management-by-obfuscation culture. Better to choose another battle to fight; one that will have on-going benefits for most after you have gone.

• Are you driven to make things better and find opposition at every twist and turn? Chances are you are fulfilling the details of your contract to the best of your ability. Is that not why they hired you in the first place? Chances are you are doing it your way because no one else seems interested. Or you do not find them capable. Or the timeline is too tight. Or it is your preferred management style. Question is: is it the right one? The answer is: obviously not in this instance.

How does this help as we fume away the hours waiting for someone to turn up to a meeting? Or nothing has been done on the new project despite it all been agreed? It helps from a point of reverse-understanding. We expend so much energy on understanding our new, foreign environment that we rarely stop and view the situation from the other perspective; how that same environment views us. You may as well be Gulliver in the land of the Lilliputians.

• You are the big boss.
• You are the unknown one.
• You may bite.
• You hold their futures in your hand.
• If you do not understand how things work, you can do serious harm to their prospects.
• Initially, until you prove otherwise, they may view you as a jumped-up pompous ass.
• If they ignore you, you may go away.
• You are disrespectful! How could anyone in your position not know what is local protocol!
• We have respect tiers here too.
• You're a nine-day wonder. We saw off your predecessor and we will see you off too.

- A foreigner is in it just for themselves.
- They use situational-awkwardness to put you in your place or challenge your calibre.

Guess what they are experiencing? They're experiencing:
- Anger flashpoints at your more audacious culture cock-ups
- I can't believe it! Did you see that! They're not on our wavelength yet.
- That's not going to happen while I'm here. Alas, this can be more a personality clash than a cultural one, and the one sure outcome of it all is, nobody wins really.

There is a lot of talk about cultural adaptation, and the need to adjust to be respectful. In every foreign/expat work situation both sides need to move towards each other in the interests of shared productivity. The narrative seems to indicate that this should be a complete adjustment otherwise there is a failure indicator. Nothing is further from the truth. A true expat exchange happens when genuine efforts are made by both sides to learn from each other, and share, respectfully. As long as you have previous experience of another culture, you cannot fully take on board another fully; in other words, if you're not Italian form birth, raised in Italy, then you can never fully be Italian. Even Italians raised the Italian way abroad exhibit differences. You carry within you your deep-rooted formative culture that you will always lead from however conscious you are of this. Neither is it desirable that we lose our beginnings or other immersive experiences completely every time we move. It is the differentness in us that makes us valuable as expats. That differentness can be vocational, as in extended expertise and qualifications; and/or it can be deeply personal and aligned with our values. The job will require the qualifications but the continued impactful success will be found in the added personal values we bring with us.

In each expat move there are recognisable cycles of adaption and integration. I call this the **Expat Adaption Cycle**. It is easy to identify where you are on your journey from the chart. The simple cycle looks like this:

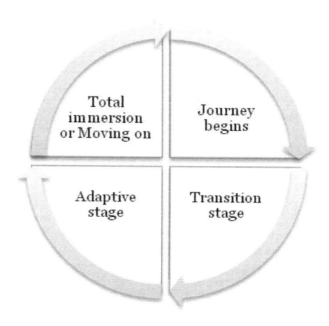

Figure 2: Expat Adaption Cycle

I have included more detail in the following chart for added clarity. The stage outcomes are indicators; elements that I have observed generally along the way.

Stage	What it means	Observable outcomes
Journey Begins	All about me	My needs My values My choices My journey
Transition Stage	6 weeks habit changes	Job adaption Lifestyle adaption Deepening cultural awareness
Adaptive Stage	Adaptive behaviour evidence	Language learning Building a new life Making new friends Integrating into expat community
Total Immersion or Moving on	Integrating into local community or end of contract	Moving easily through local community Settled in for long haul Extension of contract Or Value challenges End of contract Searching for new opportunities

Table 1: Expat Adaptive Cycle

When beliefs are challenged by experience on the ground there is a moment of personal choice. There are only two sensible outcomes: adapt and move on; stay the same and begin your search for an exit.

PERSONALITY differences are wonderful. Without them our world would be just one grey mass. Our personality is the way we bundle and deliver all the elements we have spoken about. Different personalities come in all shapes and sizes. There is no one visual that fits all. But there are certain behavioural elements that are observable wherever you find people in the world. A staff meeting is a great place to start noticing. Take the following example, for instance.

- Matthew is talking. He is shifting around in his seat, waving his hands to include everybody present, and to drive home his point. He is full of ideas. They keep tumbling out, one after the other. He always has an opinion. He begins his sentences often with, "I know what we can do,' or 'Let's do this," or 'Why don't we'. It is hard to keep track of all the balls he is throwing up in the air. Some people are switching off. Others are genuinely interested.

His contribution to the team is invaluable. Because he thinks so widely, he will often suggest something that will work. But it is up to others to do the details, and often the work afterwards too. He is an originator of ideas not a follow-through man. In fact, he will always require help with producing the goods he is so excited about.

- Ann has been listening to Matthew quietly. She is slouched down in her seat in a relaxed position, making notes. She has a thoughtful look on her face and from time to time will interrupt with a question on logistics or details. Matthew will answer frankly that he does not know yet; perhaps she, or someone else, can check it out. He is already moving onto his next idea, passing the responsibility buck smoothly. Ann is not put off; she likes what she likes. As Matthew rattles on she begins checking the internet for details and deftly puts together a spreadsheet for serious consideration. No decision will be made on anything Matthew suggests without her considered input at a later meeting. She will work the figures and the options simultaneously. She will also track any developing strategies and actions to see they deliver within budget. She makes Matthew's ideas real.

• Greg is pushed back from the table so he can stretch his legs. He thinks meetings like this are a waste of time. He would have the damn job done now if only Matthew would shut up and they could get on with it! He folds his arms across his chest and breathes in through his nose noisily. Ann is dismayed. She senses he is brewing for a confrontation; any minute now he will cut across Matthew and ask what the purpose of the meeting is, and if he really needs to be there, and he does not agree with Matthew anyway. He looks with scorn at Ann for encouraging the fool. Does she not know it will only mean more work for everybody but Matthew? He checks his phone visibly. If he leaves now he will get the waiting task done swiftly. Ann takes the lead to prevent this. He may get the job done quickly but he will not have all the details. And she knows redoing something is much harder than getting it right in the first place. And Greg rarely redoes anything without a battle. He does not see the subtle differences but he is a great worker, properly guided. He just wants to get on with things.

• Alice is sitting quietly taking it all in. She was so still Ann would think she was asleep if she was not sitting upright on the edge of her chair. Matthew was doing what he does best: spout ideas. Ann was doing what she did best: recording, analysing, logistics. Greg was thinking that if he got out of the damn meeting he would get to do what he did best: work! Get the job done while everyone else was talking and thinking about it! Alice was doing what she did best: processing everything internally to see the bigger picture for everyone. Currently she was processing what this might mean for Angie who worked a split shift every Tuesday and Thursday. When Ann asked her opinion on a logistical point, she was stumped. Matthew smirked. Greg tapped his fingers on the table waiting for Alice to say, 'I'll have to think about that and get back to you.' Ann will wait for her response. She knows it will be considered. She knows Alice is fully committed. She knows with all the details on the table, Alice's input will pay dividends for everyone. She thinks in a more disciplined way in her head than Matthew talks out loud. But Ann knows she needs them all on her team. Without all these different elements, the business would not be half as good as it is.

In a foreign environment Matthew may be seen alternatively as the best thing ever because he is so involved and will make decisions quickly, or the worst headache ever because he has no substance behind his suggestions. This is someone else's job to deliver. Some expats are recruited for this ability to think up ideas. Some are viewed with admiration because they are so loquacious. This plays directly to Matthew's extrovert personality. Problems arise when the ideas person cannot deliver the additional job parts delivered by Ann, Greg, and Alice put together. Matthew will likely deflect his inability to produce the goods onto someone else.

Ann may be seen as a rather dull and quiet leader in comparison with Matthew. Her ability to work the figures and plan logistically is impressive, as are her people management skills. She works best from behind the scenes. She is not interested in high profiling and social imaging. She lets her work record speak for itself. People come to trust her, to rely on her. They begin backing her. Ultimately her success may be her downfall as she can be seen as a threat. She depersonalises confrontation, citing her analysis. Her sensitivity to others is a plus to picking up on the unspoken; a minus if she lets the emotions around situations sway her.

Greg presents a ruthlessness he does not really have. In his kinesthetic world he just wants to get the work done. In leadership, he will make hard decisions with impunity, something that may be greatly admired in some business situations. He will get the job done quickly, and it will be 90% right. If people do not like it, they can leave. Or he will sack them anyway. He respects quick, confrontational solutions but will do his own thing anyway. The difficulty in the long term is, he is a lone ranger. He leads from the front but does not have the patience for training for sustainability. Who can do it his way anyway? In truth, nobody.

Alice impresses with her stillness and in-depth knowledge. She is considered and polite. In her introvert world it will take her longer to develop her programs but the outcome will be inclusive and sustainable. She will be undeterred from searching for the best course outcome. She may appear distant and unengaged; this is her processing internally how all will come together for the best outcome. She will meet confrontation head-on if needs be, but prefers a considered, collegial, respectful long-term outcome.

In reality, there is a lot of one of these characters in each of us, plus a decent helping of one other, and a little of the others or not. Knowing where you lead from is very valuable; knowing what is expected of you is even more valuable. Can you step up and develop a sub area? Of course you can, and it may be the making of you. Or it may bounce your stress levels off the roof as you try to fit a 'Matthew' profile into your 'Alice' personality, or vice versa. In the long term, we work from our strengths. Trying to be someone we are not will be counter-productive. A good manager will recognise this.

Note: these personality examples help us understand some age-old social anomalies. Matthew loves socialising. He needs an audience. Ann likes to relax in comfortable surroundings. A night in with good food and select company will recharge her batteries. Greg needs sports; anything with action where he can work off the edginess and pit himself against a robust opponent or opponents. He will play to win. Alice needs quietness and solitude to replenish her batteries - and a trusted friend.

There is one expat situation in particular where these general descriptions of personality differences can benefit understanding, and that is international education where staff work and socialise together, sometimes exclusively. There is no other business where the number of expats working together is so high. While Matthew recharges his batteries with frequent social events, many to the pub, for Alice, this can be hell on earth. More on this later in **Chapter 23: Opportunity of a lifetime or hell on earth**

GENDER differences in the workplace are loaded with emotion whether it is about who gets the job; differences in pay; support and advancement; and lots more. Here, I want to talk about how gender roles play out in the workplace.

For **HIM**, work is a seductive mistress. She demands his complete devotion. She can own him, body and soul. In return, she gives him **FIVE FREEDOMS** which he buys into completely:

- Freedom of self-actualisation. She helps him become all he can be in the form of all she wants him to be.
- Freedom of self-esteem. His self-worth is like an ivy plant curling around her, being affirmed and sustained by her. The more he embraces her, the more she seduces him.
- Freedom of living. She remunerates his efforts so he can live the life he wants to. The more remuneration he desires, the more he will need to give her.
- Freedom of identity. She provides his national or international identity. He defines himself in relation to her. Life without her is unthinkable.
- Freedom of choice. Being around her he finds opportunities for change. He is able to self-determine his future with regard to her; always her first.

It is these Freedoms that retirees miss the most. Having given her the best years of his life she now transfers her attentions to another. He goes through all the grief and anger and hopelessness stages of a work-divorce. She may give him a lump sum to help ease his path, and maintenance in the form of a pension. But he will never see her again. The ivy plant of his self-worth runs dry and drops to the ground.

A new devotee will push all the boundaries of his personal life to prove his worth to his new mistress. She just soaks it all up and asks for more. Sometimes she withholds her Freedoms if her new lover does not fawn at her feet all the time. It is impossible to gauge how much is enough. Her Freedoms are too important to forfeit though. And everybody else is clamouring for her attention. It is easy to see where accompanying spouses and family fit in in this scenario. In short, they don't. Often, they don't understand. Feeding the work-mistress; cajoling the work-mistress, is the single most potent point of conflict within expat families.

A seasoned expat will be respectful of his new mistress. He too will give all he can but hopefully he has learned that she can be fickle, selfish and utterly demanding as well as being incredibly generous. He will go into this new relationship with his eyes open. But regardless of all experience of dealing with ladies like this his entire life, he will be seduced into keeping her company constantly. How many husbands keep their mistress their side of the bed in the form of their iPhone? How many wives have heard her demanding voice in the middle of the night; at the weekend; and on the beach? How many can say they have control of their work life? How many find that their work-mistress is all they have left after an expat move?

The big question around all this is: is work the primary force in life or is living the primary force in work?

For **HER**, work is a friend. He is a port in a storm; ships in which she can sail her dreams while making his come true. She shares her life and her expertise with him and in return he gives her **FIVE POWERS**:

- Power to self-actualise. She can professionally become all she can be within the confines of his job.
- Power for self-esteem. She draws her work confidence and validation from him.
- Power for living. He provides her with the money she needs to live her life in work and outside.

- Power for identity. She draws her work identity from the job she is doing, whether national or international.
- Power for choice. She can take the expertise she has developed with him and apply it in numerous other ways.

When she retires, she takes these Powers with her. She has Powers in other areas of her life too. She makes use of them all. There is no work-divorce although there are many separations along the way.

Meeting a true new friend can take time. There are many false friends out there for her; ones that will try and push her in the wrong direction; ones that will try to exploit her; ones that will only see her in one role. She is looking for that something that will make a difference in her life. It may be money but it may not be too. She is fully prepared to give all that is necessary to succeed. Sometimes she has to give more than her male counterpart. But she measures it better. And she can be just as ruthless as the next one if needs be though this is likely to cost her more in the long run!

A seasoned expat is looking for a partnership with a friend. She remains flexible yet is measured in approach and accomplishment. This work friend has a fixed place in regards to her personal life. He may be a large part of her life, for example, his east to her west; they tangent but do not overlap. Her purpose of working is to have a life. He respects and admires this.

The question here is: is earning a living synonymous with living a life?

At the end of any expat job, take the time to consider these additional questions:

- Who are you now?
- Where are you off to now?
- How are you doing?
- Are you **2G** happy: happy with what you have **GIVEN** and happy with what you have **GAINED**?

14

EPILOGUE: FAMILY MATTERS

MY FAMILY MATTER to me hugely yet here I was half way around the world without them. It didn't make sense; yet it made perfect sense, all at the same time. It's the expat family dilemma. I have seen it time and again in my many moves as well as experiencing it first-hand. A move away benefited all of us; extended us globally; provided access and opportunity where none or not so much was available before. A beautifully packaged sentence but not the whole story. Feelings and emotions have a way of creeping out through the seams of the package and suddenly the BIG DEAL doesn't seem so big any more. It has lost weight per distance travelled.

We left our young adult children behind; we left our parents and siblings behind. We took a chance and it paid off. We made it pay off. And it worked out well in the end. But there were rocky days; lonely days, and even lonelier weekends. Our complete family unit was a whole lot of fun. We challenged each other in the best ways possible. We laughed and played together. We hugged a lot. We argued. We said, 'I'm sorry.' We said, 'I love you'. We relaxed in each other's company. We looked out for each other. We encouraged each other. We helped each other. And we missed this. And so did they. But it was exactly all this that made the separation work. Funny, the contradictions in living that make living work.

Our son and daughter came to visit and they loved our new life. They experienced a different way of living and they were able to dream bigger. They caught our dream and made it their own. Our family love magnet pulled us closer; kept us close that first move, and since. There was nothing we could do to make this happen except be there welcoming them to our new home. They had to make their individual responses to the new environment and decide if it really was worthwhile and indeed, what the fuss was about to warrant the separation anyway. We were ecstatic when they fell in love with Tokyo as much as we did. We were validated in our hopes and dreams that our personal move would benefit all of us.

Our extended family worried for us. During our time in Tokyo we experienced earthquakes regularly. If fact, if we didn't we would worry that a big one would happen! We had some sizeable ones that made the walls creak and the buildings sway both at home and at work. This was something we had to fathom out as a matter of urgency. We had to crack this country's environmental procedures asap. Our physical survival depended on it. Our families were on high alert for us. They called us as soon as any earthquake news was announced internationally. Some knew exactly the geographical location of the quake; others, whose geography was as general as mine, would not. Some remembered the time difference; some did not. And when a volcano erupted in the ring of fire we were remembered more intensely. They had got used to the regularity of the earthquakes to be faced with another unknown worry for us. We were grateful for their calls. It was lovely to be remembered. But I think it scared off any possible visitors. And we were a long way away and costly to visit. And not many were interested in wrestling with so-foreign a culture. And when we returned home to visit they breathed a sigh of relief and wanted us to stay. Some were more interested than others in our journeys. Some had no point of reference at all to chat with us about our new life and retreated into the safety of thinks known, local events. We learned to move with the flow and meet people on their ground. They were still interested in us, just not where we had been. Our journey was a closed door; it only chinked open a fraction to let out a small bit of light. Too much blinded people into silence. We had to learn to share our present moments without our past enrichments.

Working internationally is full of challenges. Initially we focussed on the home culture and missed the richness of other cultures that inhabited the workplace. Others English speakers found our accent clear but our idiom difficult to figure out unless they had worked with Irish people beforehand. We had difficulty in telling Australian, New Zealand, and South African accents apart; and we even had similar issues with US and Canadian accents too. Our local Japanese hosts were perplexed at times that English could sound so different. But they had their dialects too, their accents, and those we never got to understand as we strove to learn the 'school' Japanese that was taught to foreigners.

Language was only one issue that we had to concern ourselves with. Leadership and management styles differed with continents, and teaching strategies and content was often as individual as nationality and all had to be streamlined to the curriculum at hand. It was a great learning milieu! I gleaned tips and resources that I had not known of previously and was able to share what I knew in return. When you work in an area you love it is easy to overspend time there and I did. After a while there was a diminishing return on all the extra stuff and fatigue clouded excitement. I was doing what the majority of other expats were doing; I was over involved. There was a safety net in all of this too. The more time I spent in work, and work environment, the less I was challenged by daily living. My friends were my workmates. I was living the bubble life. And bubbles *always burst. Then it is time to regroup or move on. Most times it is just easier to move on. Sometimes it is necessary and we are the last to see it.*

PART 3
SOCIAL LIVING

"You can make more friends in two months by becoming interested in other people than you can in two years by trying to get other people interested in you."

Dale Carnegie, How to Win Friends and Influence People

15

PROLOGUE: SOCIAL LIVING

IN THE REALM of the deeply personal we find the focus can often be around others or a specific other, and the milieu in which we find them. This part of our lives plays out in the bubble of social living that is the expat life. In the beginning, the group of people we socialise with can be small. We may have no alternative but to join this party if we are to have any life outside work or the home. We may continue to socialise with this group out of loyalty even when the misfit signs are flashing red for us to see or it may truly have all the elements we need at that moment and we see no need to broaden our friendship base. This is me in expat land seeking meaningful connection.

Me, me, me

These **3 Me's** provide significant challenges in our expat bubble lives:

- **Me + others:** this is me in my drive for meaningful communication. I want me to matter. I want to see and be seen. I want to share my life with others in an altruistic and reciprocally beneficial manner. I need a friend, or friends. I need human contact at different levels. I need this to assuage the barrenness of existence I find myself in. I want people in my life I can have fun with; be challenged by and challenge in return; to chat to; to share a cup of coffee with; to dull the monotony of the monochrome life and bring in colour in all its glory.

- **Me + one significant other:** This is me in my drive for deep personal connection. I want to touch and be touched at heart level. I want to walk hand in hand with someone I can love and respect and who loves and respects me back. I want to see life through this one other's eyes and let him or her see through mine. I want to relax in trust in private, to shut out the world and be at peace.

- **Me + beggars:** This is me at my most vulnerable. I share no enjoyment with these people. Instead they pluck at my heartstrings as well as my pocket and I know I cannot make it right for them. I am so guilty inside but I am strong and cold on the outside. Or I am so guilty inside and I am unerringly gullible on the outside. And I am afraid. I am afraid of them and I am afraid for them. And I am afraid for me. I just don't know how to get it right but I know I must keep me safe first. I want to look after all of them but I don't know how. I need to discern the genuine from the organised. Sometimes I get it right; often I get it wrong. It reveals more about me to myself than I am really comfortable with. Often it reveals misplaced guilt.

Part 3 delves into the personal realm; an area often ignored or moved down the priority list when moving to live abroad. We are deeply feeling creatures and it is hard to make sense of what is happening in our lives in this emotionally charged, or barren, overseas location. We have to find solutions to ourselves, our aloneness, our loneliness, our desires, our wants, to our need for connection to ensure we really are ok. And more often than not, we will have to find a way to deal with being targeted by beggars.

16

A NECKLACE OF FRIENDS

MY FIRST EXPAT move was from Dublin to Old Windsor. Our children were 9 and 7. Ireland was in deep recession and you were lucky to get a money job let alone a career one. My husband had a job as a teacher but the profession was over-subscribed; there were no more teaching jobs for the newly qualified, like me. And the newly qualified were over-qualified for the few money jobs that were available. No one wanted to hire a graduate who would quit at the first sniff of a professional start. We were struggling to meet the mortgage; discouraged by the years ahead on a tight budget.

My husband was the first to propose we go overseas. He had turned down the offer of a Green Card[10] shortly after we were married as we wanted our children to grow up in proximity to family. Now they were older we both felt that some time overseas would be beneficial for all of us. We could see the world first-hand and maybe claw our way out of the financial hole we were experiencing.

---

[10] A Green Card gives you the right to work in the US.

In Ireland, my friendships revolved around family and a few close neighbour friends, and some from university I saw ever more infrequently. These were easy-going, spontaneous relationships that did not stand on formality. I was never lonely. And the only isolation I experienced was when the children had chickenpox.

Old Windsor, Windsor, Runnymede, Englefield Green, are all wonderful places. St John's Beaumont, my husband's new school, was a revelation, an olde world apart, standing firmly on best Jesuit practices. School until 6:00pm, which included homework time, and a half day on a Saturday, became the way the world was for our son. He thrived on the opportunities and quickly made friends with a small cohort of boys who remain best mates to this day. They were his surrogate brothers, and family, he spent so much time in their company. My husband lived his work. He loved the environment, the outside-the-box thinking of his young boss, the drive to succeed that emanated from the place.

St Cuthbert's, the local girls school, sadly did not provide anything similar for our daughter who missed Ireland and her friends intensely. She never did make friends at this school but was plagued by bullying which followed her quiet, academic demeanour for years. We removed her within the year and she came to school with me; by this time I had realised my dream and was teaching nearby. She found herself again, and made one firm friend who stood by her until university separated them many years later.

And, as usual, I put myself last. It's an occupational and living hazard with trailing spouses. We moved in mid August and as is common with every move, you just know yourselves or yourself and a contact from work. And as is common, the HR Department was excellent at getting us settled, particularly my husband, and son, since he would be going to the same school. My daughter and I were offered advice but we were outside the wall, as it were. All energies were focused on, and around, the employee. My husband had the car, the career, the National Insurance Number, the bank account. I *had all day. After I walked my daughter to school I was on my own. In one fell swoop I lost my home, my family, my friends, my husband, my son, my identity, my self-esteem. I had entered the land of the invisible; the land of the expat trailing spouse. My salvation came in the form of a kind parent at my daughter's school. Simply, she **SAW** me, and she offered me a lift to school as I had yet to get my own car. Mary was my first expat friend; the first jewel in my necklace of friends around the world.*

It only takes one friend to make a world of difference.

One of the joys of expat living is meeting new people from all over the world, locals and expats alike. Expats are initially more likely to seek out friendship among their home language group or within their language capabilities. Their first port of call will be the workplace. For some, this will be a large, rich vein; for others, it may be a link of one or two. But that is all that is needed at first to help deal with the strangeness of a new place. In every country I have worked I have found the local people genuinely supportive and helpful but they are not on my wavelength initially; neither am I on theirs. An evening in the company of a similarly travelled expat provides relief from continuous cultural adjustment; it provides mental down-time, and mental down-time provides much needed relaxation.

When you arrive in your new country you will make the most of the same-language friendship pool you find immediately around you whether you are going out to work, looking after the family from home or on your own at home. If you are working with a large group of expats, you have new-friendship choices. If you are a single expat among locals and do not speak the language yet, you may struggle to make a friend. Similarly as a trailing spouse with or without children: where will you find friends? And how?

You will find friends at/through:
- The school or kindergarten your children go to

- Universities or colleges you may take courses at
- Among your spouse's colleagues and families
- Professional organisations
- Community centres
- Clubs
- Language schools, centres, or lessons
- Gyms and leisure centres
- Recreational courses and seminars of interest
- Pubs
- Events
- Personal introduction

The list is indicative only; there are many ways you can meet new people. I am sure you can add many more venues and opportunities from your personal experience.

The how is simple; I do not necessarily mean easy as at some time or another you will have to force yourself to:

- Wake up
- Get out of bed
- Shower
- Dress
- And get out the door!

If you get through this to the street, on a bad day, you may baulk at the transport process; the inevitable 'Scooby[11]' as we so lovingly called

---

[11] A 'Scooby' is defined by Scooby Doo's exclamation of surprise. It is experienced after you get into a taxi, give the directions, and your taxi driver delivers a 'Scooby' of misunderstanding. Once a fellow traveller shared this with me, all my frustration at being misunderstood disappeared and I began to look forward to my 'Scooby' moments. I went 18 months in Shanghai without having one only to meet 3 in one week - to my delight. I put this down to 3 possible things: my language learning is following an inverse curve, I am actually getting worse; the driver is Shanghaise, he speaks an almost completely different language; the driver isn't interested in trying to fathom out where this incoherent foreigner is going, he's ready for his tea.

it in Shanghai; the security checks at Metro Line 10; or just taking your life in your hands as you attempt to cross the road at the green man or pedestrian crossing. When you are down, everything is an uphill struggle, but it is worth it. The one thing that will make life easier for you is time with a fellow-traveller; the moment you begin to reach out is the first step to freedom in this new land. One way forward is to join everything or at least one thing that will begin the going-out habit. Sometimes the expense of doing a lot initially can be prohibitive as you have drained the bank account with all the moving pay-outs but do try and leave something for that first month until the first pay check has come in because this is exactly when you need that 'out' the most; that something for you that is not finding out where to buy beans and shampoo and bananas. A month later, inertia may have set in along with the depression and it will be harder to move.

HOW specifics:
• Take people up on invitations. Expats and locals are generous. They genuinely want you to be happy in this new location.
• Introduce yourself at gatherings. Ask for advice. Network. Every successful person around you started from the same place as you. Nobody is a mind reader and expats always put their best face forward. No one will know you are hurting unless you tell them. Everyone hurts at one time or another on an expat move. Sometimes expats carry incalculable emotional distress around with them, pushing it down deeper and deeper with every move until the dam breaks. This often manifests as various malaises, persistent and stubbornly resistant to treatments until the root causes are dealt with. But at a first glance you would never know.
• Offer your services for free initially. Whatever you can do – tutor, event plan, write, make music, cook, interior design, etc. – begin to do it where you now find yourself. Take the crumbs on offer.

One, they may be all that you can get; and two, they may lead to the opportunity of a lifetime.

• Start up a chat with other expats in coffee shops, pubs, restaurants or at least smile and ask if the food or drink is ok or for directions somewhere. The person you are addressing may be as eager as you for conversation.

• Take a class around an existing or new interest. See where it leads. At any rate it will keep your mind occupied and will provide you with new material to chat to your partner about.

• Join professional groups. They may meet infrequently, and not everything they do will be your cup of tea, but they will encourage and challenge you to get the most out of where you are. Be open to what sparks your interest. Be prepared to share your curiosity. The people you meet here are successful professionals looking for friendships too. Your journeys will be remarkably similar. Simply by sitting in the same room as them their enthusiasm for life and learning will rub off on you.

• Have your own goals. Schedule your day. Get up in the morning, every morning.

• Consider retraining. Take a diploma, degree, masters or doctorate online. Plan on leaving with something more than you arrived. Plan on leaving with something country-independent, language-independent, and partner-job independent.

You will likely experience a variety of friends in your new move: they are all necessary; all have their place in your new life. In many ways this is no different than moving from London to Liverpool. The dynamic and process is the same underneath those layers of added complexity called 'other language' and/or 'other culture'. But unlike the friends you expect to make in London or Liverpool, same language expats all over the world are rarely only what their passport say they are. You are likely interacting with a multi-cultural mind wrapped up in a national package. Don't expect that because they are Irish that they will like Guinness, and have it for breakfast!

In my expat journeys I have met both people who work and people who remain at home, who have had:

- Coffee friends
- Tennis club friends
- Drinking friends
- Colleague friends
- Social friends
- Sex friends
- Partners
- Spouses
- Best friends
- Soul friends
- Church friends
- Friends for a season
- And many others, the list is too long to mention every category!

These friends have either:

- Encouraged
- Uplifted
- Challenged and supported them to be all they can be
- Are amazingly altruistic

Or they have masqueraded as friends who:

- Criticized
- Dragged them down
- Become dependent
- Are stuck
- Are dysfunctional

- Are full of themselves
- Are needy
- Are intolerant
- Are loud
- Are noisy
- Are acquisitive

It is hard initially to differentiate the 'glass half full' from the 'glass half empty' when you desperately need the chance to hear yourself talking to someone else; and to be heard by someone else. The hope is that they will recognise you for the person you are; that you will be SEEN by another soul, and your presence in this new place validated as a result. That said, it is sometimes easier to spend time with those who have issues with where they are than face the prospect of doing something for yourself with the encouraging bunch. It is okay to retreat and lick your wounds but if you are several months into your posting and you are embedded with the 'finding fault' group and they show no sign of moving on, it is time to recognise that these people are most likely like this wherever they are in the world, the new move has only give them more steam. That is your moment of choice. What you do after that will define the success of this move or not. If you decide to change your thinking at this point, you can truly change your life.

I have a simple two-part code of living. Firstly, wherever I am in the world I am either working or learning. For the majority of our expat life I have worked outside the home. I have taught in primary and middle schools; I have managed IT networks; I have trained teachers in IT systems and curricula integration. I have taken course after course to be the best I can be while working; location based and through distance learning. In my previous location, the only long term one as a trailing spouse, I have retrained as an NLP life coach because I see it as the difference that makes the difference in helping people achieve their dreams. From my experience as an IT trainer, qualifications alone don't always make the difference if people don't believe in their own head that they can make it happen. It is this self-belief that is seriously challenged as a trailing spouse. Not everyone is entrepreneurial. Believe I can make 'what' happen, I hear regularly. Many trailing spouses have tons of belief; what they lack is the legal opportunity to contribute to society and their personal purse through meaningful work. Language can be the second barrier. Thinking outside the box is a skill that can be learned. If you change your thinking around a difficulty, you can change your life. It ultimately comes down to choice. How badly do you want it?

Secondly, I work, and give, to empower people. People are the world. Do I always get it right? Hardly! I'm only human. And sometimes I shy away from making friends because there's always a leaving point as an expat; either they leave or I do, and it's painful, and lonely all over again because no two friends are alike. No one can fill the shoes of another. And it is this exact dilemma that makes the journey and investment together so worthwhile when we do meet new people. Plus I don't believe in coincidences. I believe each person comes into my life for a purpose; and me theirs. That tangential moment in time is precious in the support role we bring to each other.

WORK FRIENDS: There is a tendency to seek friends initially from within the job. This is natural and to be expected. You share so much in common already by working in the same place, and it is often unlikely that you will have much time to find friends outside work in the beginning. Then after a while inertia sets in and you settle to these friendships only; they become an identity for you; you are part of a recognisable group. Expectations of, and responsibilities to, the group sets in. You support each other. You look out for each other. You seek out and cultivate new members to the group. Such a strong friendship group can become incestuous and limiting. It can also impinge on best work practices: the buddy vote can sway development in the workplace. Dissension within the group can be felt on the work floor. Exclusion from the group can be disastrous from a career, as well as a friendship, viewpoint. Inclusion can stop people from moving on; from seeking out a different perspective; from making individual friendships. The group identity can perpetuate unhelpful habits, e.g. excessive drinking, smoking, promiscuity. This group identity can hold you as firmly as any strong family values. If this is your choice, great. If not, seek out other friendships. Look to your reasons for living the expat life.

The friendship needs you have as an expat when you first arrive in a new place will be driven by your fears and insecurities around the move, the drive to avoid isolation, and financial consolidation. You are happy to, and need to, group together. You cannot afford to be as selective as you normally are. You herd together in survival mode. But this will change as you progress through the weeks and years. It is only natural that you will seek out new, additional friendship connections around your new way of thinking. Some of your original friends will move with you, others will not. Friendships are made and let go of continuously. People bring with them their individual ways and habits around friendships. Expat living exacerbates the negative. Controlling behaviour patterns become more intense in a smaller pool of friends. Expat living pushes the positive. You have to be a friend to make a friend. Deep friendships formed this way can last forever.

> The friendship needs you have as an expat when you first arrive in a new place will be driven by your fears and insecurities around the move, the drive to avoid isolation, and financial consolidation.

There is a tendency for trailing spouses to identify with a partner's work-colleague friends too if this is their only option for making friends. This can be beneficial, and alternatively, it can be awkward.

With my husband in a leadership position at work, it is problematic at times to have friends within his workforce, or spouse work-friends. Not everyone can differentiate the person from the job, and with certain people I have to be more private than I would prefer to be. Some people just cannot but pass on information; others naturally keep a confidence to keep a friend. Some cultivate me for the very purpose of information, or from the perceived job benefit my time with them bestows. As if! So I have all sorts of friends. I turn away nobody. I know from experience that the best way to make a friend is to be a friend. I am my own person. So is he.

Here are some more jewels in my expat necklace of friends: Marie, Kevin, Nicole, Perry, Joan, Chris, Marie, Johnny, Winnie, Jenny, Tony, Monica, Barbara, Brendan, John, Mary, Ray, Bernie.

Sometimes work friends can become more than friends. Sex in the workplace can make everyday team work uncomfortable, and not irregularly, downright awkward. Finding the man or woman of your dreams while working abroad does happen but for every successful partnership begun in this way are many more lonely and sexually frustrated single people, both single as in unattached, or single as in working away from a spouse for months on end. Sex matters. And sometimes because it is not available through traditional relationships, it is all one can think of. And sometimes, sex happens because people change norms when in a different country.

Some of my most uncomfortable moments working as an expat came from working in an environment where two predatory men competed to sleep their way around the female staff. This flowed over to adolescent behaviour such as sex in the toilets and around the building. One supervisor was held to ransom in a staff meeting by her lover who publicly deflected criticism over his poor work performance onto the colour of her knickers.

What you do sexually as an adult expat is your choice and responsibility. When it spills over into the workplace, like the previous paragraph, it becomes everybody's responsibility. Personally I resent this intrusion into professional life. Leave your immaturity at Immigration on the way in.

Friendships do evolve into something more intimate, beautiful and long-lasting too. These friendships have depth and authenticity. There are many mature expats who deal with this in a private manner taking cognisance of the feelings of others. Their joy and happiness permeates the workplace. It gives everyone a lift. Expat living can make it easier for same-sex couples to live together, culture permitting, although it is still possible for these couples to experience prejudice from other expats. Expat living is a microcosm of the world's tolerances and prejudices. The primary key to successful workplace relationships is discretion. The second is maturity. The third is respect; respect for each other and for your colleagues.

Sometimes friendships evolve that are difficult to defend: casual sex partners; multi sex partners; sexual harassment; infidelity; affairs. Sex is never an isolated event for women; there is always an emotional investment or sadly maybe a career investment. If not positive the fallout can be horrendous. Sex may simply be opportunistic for a man. A man leader ousted in sexual activity weathers the storm much more easily than a female leader caught in a similar situation. He is just sowing his wild oats; she is a whore. Perception around an event is often much more potent than what actually happened. Life happens. In an expat bubble community all emotions are sharper. This is the buzz and the burnout that expats have such a love/hate relationship with.

NON-WORK FRIENDS: These can be the hardest to find initially. At any rate, your friendship experience will be within the monetary tier your position commands. This has a significant impact on how you experience the culture of any post. It is not unusual to find social bullying within every tier. This may manifest as social snobbishness or just plain displeasure from not joining a drinking clique; ultimately you may find yourself side-lined and isolated. This speaks more to the controlling and needy side of the perpetrator. There is nothing that says all expats are lovely people. Some are the meanest you will find anywhere in the world. All that has changed in their world is the location. Expat living enhances both personality strengths and weaknesses.

In the grey areas of life behind the excitement of a new venture and the lows of lost identity you will sadly find people who are:

- Alcoholics
- Utter narcissists
- Drug addicts
- Sex addicts
- And have a barrowful of other personal issues.

Expat life chews up those who have no support group; who lose their self-esteem in the move; who lose their partners to the work-mistress or a work love-mistress; particularly those who do not want to be there or who are there to nobly 'support the man if they cannot support the plan'. They wander the landscape in a haze of aloneness; invisible and unhappy. They drink; have affairs; overspend; or escape into a drug haze. What they are saying is:

- It is your fault I am here
- You are to blame for my unhappiness
- I can't do anything
- I will make you pay.

What is really happening is that they have abdicated responsibility for their life to someone else. There are many models of dependency. The best one is the one that is actively worked out, and reviewed, with your partner. None demands you give up your freedom of choice. You always have that. Always. Isolation can mess with your head. Isolation within the loving partnership that brought you both to this place can be destructive if not acknowledged and overcome. Sometimes the only real escape can be the one to leave the relationship completely if you were not so dependent, or if it were not to impact negatively on the children. Hands up if you have thought like this in your vulnerable moments! It is an entirely natural response to a lack of meaning in your current position. You do not have to be an expat to experience moments of despondency like these. But as an expat, half-way around the world, your options are different, more challenged, your support group small or non-existent, and that is not even going to the difficult cultural countries where a woman only exists as an adjunct to a man or a man is not a real man unless he is the breadwinner. Trailing spouses, both men and women, more often than not, turn to destructive habits to get them through the day and night, rather than admit failure in their personal relationships, or negatively impact the high-flyer partner's perception in his or her workplace. Put 'over' before any regular activity and you have the beginning of a destructive habit: overeating, oversleeping, overtraining, overdrinking; etc. excess habits that punish the body to quiet the mind. It takes longer for love to die than you think. Sometimes the financial benefits can overcome infidelity as sexual practices change with location and opportunity. You get to choose what you can deal with as part of your personal relationship. Do you really believe that your self-worth is as valuable as your partner's? We all measure self-worth differently. How do you define that self-worth in your relationship? Is being here in this place, with this person, building up my self-worth or eroding it? And – how much responsibility am I taking for my own self-worth?

A friendship is a wonderful thing. Friends can help in a way no lover can. We are all multifaceted people. No one person can reflect back to us all of our wonderfulness. We are like a precious gemstone with many faces, many talents. Think how much more we will shine in the world if we practice being a friend as much as having a friend. The choice of your friends, and your choice of friendship, will determine how brightly you glow in the world. Playing small to remain invisible will help nobody, starting with you.

You will experience 4 different friendship phases in your expat journey:

Figure 3: Friendship phases

Phase 1: Survival friend. You have just arrived. You need someone to show you around; point you in the best direction for shopping; show you how to use the subway; take you out for a coffee. You are grateful for this 'out'. You have a survival friend. In turn, you can choose to become a survival friend to someone else.

Phase 2: Comfortable friend. You are more comfortable with one, or more, 'survival' friend. You meet now because you like to chat. You enjoy each other's company. Additionally, you can introduce these friends to other friends you have met at language classes or the gym. A pattern of friendship activities emerge, often with individual emphasis.

Phase 3: True friend. You find one friendship is becoming stronger than the other friendships. You have found a true friend. This person supports and encourages; it is a reciprocal arrangement. You begin to share your life with your friend. Your discussions move from where you can get the best bargain to life values and experiences. You still meet with your other friends. You can still be a friend to them and them, you. Some you will naturally begin to see less frequently. Some you will need to stop seeing because they are draining your energy and resources. Some dump you because you are no longer of value to them.

Phase 4: Best friend. You or your best friend leaves. Your necklace of friends around the world has begun. Your relationship will change with distance but it can continue to flourish. This is beautiful. If you have invested heavily in this friendship to the exclusion of all others in an expat environment you will feel bereft if you are the one left behind. You will have to begin your friendship journey again, in this same place, but probably with less enthusiasm now since you have already adapted to living here. If you are the one going onto a new environment you will be lonely but your focus is onward and you need to direct your energy and attention there to the survival stage again. The person remaining always feels it harder when a close friend moves away.

Friendships at work go through these phases too but in much quicker succession since people are thrown together for longer periods. There is an element of 'friends for a season' in all of these friendships. The fact that expat living is essentially transient can slow down the progress of a friendship or accelerate it. Grasp the opportunity and enjoy learning from and enjoying each other's company.

Some friendship advice:

- Recognise and honour whichever phase you are currently in. It will pass and change so make the most of it.

- Decide what **YOU** want to do, not what your work spouse/partner wants you to do. He or she may be a different personality from you. He or she may be jealous of the time you have on your hands to do whatever you want.

- Get out of the house or apartment. This is worthwhile even if you are still alone outside in the gym, shopping centre, coffee shop, pub. This is distraction. Many working spouses equate not working and having more disposable income with absolute freedom but it can be soul destroying – having money and time to go where you want, when you want, but all on your own ad infinitum. Most trailing spouses require more substance than that.

- Get out of the house or apartment to spend time with another person. This is interaction, and life is beginning to look better because of it. This may be in the form of a language lesson, a seminar, a book club, the pursuit of a hobby.
- Make connections. Be prepared to share yourself with others. Invite people to meet you for coffee sometime in a convenient coffee shop. Avoid inviting people home initially. Most expats prefer a neutral environment. Share your email details.
- If you make an appointment to meet up with someone, keep it unless you are seriously ill or genuinely have an emergency situation. It is not unusual to brave up to making an appointment and then chicken out feeling insecure about anything and everything from how to get there to what you might have to say to this person anyway.

Friendships are living lifelines; they are alive by definition and need nurturing. But do not let the busyness of friendships keep you from living your dream either. True friends will encourage and support you. If you have a friendship that is restricting you from being all you can be rethink your involvement with that person. Give yourself permission to be all you can be.

Here are some more jewels in my necklace of friends around the world: Ling, Shelley, Sophie, Simon, Andrew, Lesley, Will, Klára, Eva, Evelyn, Lape, Moses, Paul, Jana, Dave, Doreen, Ildiko, Myra, Tanya, Brett.

And our friendship jewels keep shining further and further around the globe: Jason, Sue, JoAnn, Michael, Pete, Jill, Iain, Athena, Neil, Judy, Sigrid, Jane, Tere, Jocelyn, Fran, Mark, Susan,

Michael, Trevor, Peter, Giles, Imai san, Nick, Hong, Richard, Melissa, Deborah, Anna, Colin, Ellen, the list goes on!

At its centrepiece is Martin, friend first, friend always. It is supported by two beautiful friendships with my expat children, Fionnuala and Brendan, enhanced further by their life-partners, Will and Klára. Why have children if you cannot enjoy the special friendship that only they can bring? And I have two new chains of friends in the making: my grandchildren, Siobhán, Liam, Niamh, and Maxim, and those I have yet to meet along the way. I love my friendship jewels lighting my way around the world!

17

PERSONAL RELATIONSHIPS ON THE GO

IMAGINE ALL THE expats where you live as one tribe, living apart in a fortified town or large village, all locals kept outside the wall. This group of expats are by definition non-locals although the group is made up of a mix of 'other' nationals who may or may not speak the same language. But as far as the locals are concerned, they are all the same, i.e. not local.

Expats come and go from this group. Some interact only within this group or within a subset of this group, i.e. same language groups. Most interact with as many other nationals as possible. All are thrown together as a large homogenous group of expats although it is likely that the homogeneity is related to the task in hand rather than the nationality.

Some expats join the group with partners. Most leave with the same partners. Some leave with others. Other expats join as singles from both sexes. All ages are represented. The vast majority follow the career trail or are there in a support role, i.e. trailing spouses. Initially, there is only time settling into the job and proving your worth.

Eventually there is time for relationships – those that are already in place or those that are desired, in the making, on the lookout. Many expats seek relationships from those around them, who understand them, who hold the same values. Some will look over the fence at the exotic locals and become mesmerised and enthralled. Some locals will look over the fence in at the expats and long to be part of their exotic and free lifestyle.

This village life is always changing. People come and go all the time. Some bring locals into the mix; some abandon the village for the locals. Married expats often live their lives isolated from each other, the trailing spouse immersed in the minutiae of village living while the working partner performs 24/7 for the business. Their relationships become like parallel train tracks with an aspirational happy life at the end of it all. Similarly for working partners; even if they work for the same company their roles and teams will be different. Again, parallel train-track lives. Locational relationships can become more meaningful or the opportunity to take flirtation to its ultimate goal desirable. Expat work situations provide opportunities for personal relationships.

Single men may find it awkward or easy to develop desirable personal relationships depending on the village. Some may not be looking for a relationship; they may be escaping heartache or destructive habits but in time the loneliness will encroach and they may or may not find what they are looking for. Some have poor social skills; some attract partners like giant magnets, often locals. Some will see any resulting relationships as transitory; there are always other fish in the sea, right? Others really want to meet that special one and create a family. All will be cognisant of their transitory international work situation. Money matters can become more serious or it is time to escape again.

Single women have the worst deal with personal relationships abroad. Women are not as promiscuous as men although their sex drive is no less so. I have seen many brothels in my overseas postings; they exist everywhere – for men! I have yet to see one single unit visibly marketed to women. Plus women have a ticking fertility clock which ticks louder and more aggressively with each passing year. Age matters more for women seeking relationships internationally, as does specific cultures. Some expat males prey on the isolation and loneliness of women to get them into bed. Some women succumb. But it is fair to say that the vast majority of women see sex in a different way than men; and relationships too. Women have to consider trust more around relationships. Sometimes the expat pool of available men is not ready to be trustworthy partners in a long term relationship. Sometimes both expat single men and women do not see expat living as a place to commit to a lifelong relationship. Some relationships started overseas may continue into distance relationships. What happens then is often uncertain.

I have seen very lonely single people in my expat journeys. These are wonderfully sensitive and caring people but they are alone. Some drink excessively to numb the loneliness; some herd together for social protection. Some men frequent brothels even if it means they will be deported if found. Some have a fear of commitment or have been stung emotionally before. Many women are heartbroken about lost opportunities for having a family. Many are sad and regretful about not having even been asked out on a date.

I have seen very lonely partners in my expat journeys. They are running on the train tracks, apart but at least in the same direction, and the lines still tangent in the distance. This expat village can be a very delusional place.

Locals can be really caught up in relational exploits in the expat village too in four particular ways:

1. They can meet and enter into a terrific lifelong relationship with an expat who respects and loves them.

2. They can be used by expats.
3. They can use expats as a ways out or a leg up the ladder.
4. Their working alongside expats can make them unsuitable for a local partner. Because of their expat experience they think differently and develop different expectations. They may never marry as a consequence.

Expats do not inhabit an isolated village within any city of course, nor anyplace else for that matter. But the analogy helps introduce the situational experiences around personal relationships that exist wherever expats and locals interact.

You know what personal relationships are. We all know what personal relationships are. And we know they can be tricky, not just at the beginning but at every twist and turn throughout life. And as much as we know they can be tricky we know they play a tremendous part in how happy and fulfilled we feel. Personal relationships are about how we feel together, how good we feel together. And how awful we feel when things go wrong. Personal relationships lift life out of the logical, the measurable. At the core of our feelings is the need to be loved and to love; to give and receive at a depth of humility and surrender that is as frighteningly fragile as it is sublimely beautiful; the total gift of one to the other. Additionally, personal relationships can be about family, about extending the family line to another generation. But first and foremost it is about attraction and sex. We don't have to think about how this works in our home environment. Our responses have been conditioned from childhood. But overseas can be another story altogether. 'Personal relationships on the go' perch precariously on the pillars of culture, communication, and work/non-work.

CULTURE is the invisible, unspoken determinant on how and if relationships between expats, and between expats and locals exist and/or flourish. The how and why of cultural practice runs deep in communities; we are all outcomes of cultural determination. Culture exists to keep us safe from outsiders and other identifiable and unidentifiable threats. It exists for family and community continuity and sustainability. But underneath all cultural umbrellas humans are similar; all need the same nourishment and care to live; all need protection from the elements; all need ways of self-determination and sustenance. The 'what' is the same; the 'how' it is achieved varies locally.

Some cultures are open to cross-cultural relationships, some closed. Some define feminine beauty in a way that makes it difficult for other-culture women to get a date let alone enter into a relationship with a local man. Some local men avoid expat women not because of their 'other beauty' but because of their 'other mindset'; these women are too independently minded, they will not take care of their men in the way they have been accustomed to. Religious mindsets play a huge role here too. Submissiveness may be anything from attractive to compulsory in a female mate but it is unlikely that any expat woman would have that as top of her 'to be' list.

Expat men may find it easier to form short-term and long-term relationships in most cultures but there are those in particular that they need to be very circumspect in, and out of respect leave the local women alone. These are the times when men must decide with their head rather than their genitals should they wish to leave the country intact. Conversely, men may well find themselves the prey, the ticket out or the leg up the ladder. Older men in managerial roles are of particular interest as they have the power to elevate a career and the money to pay for a mistress. Many of these lonely men are working 'alone' in a new place having left their families at home for the duration.

Sex within the expat life is a thorny issue. Sex matters, perhaps even more, as an expat for two reasons – its extreme availability and its extreme absence, both of local determination. Couple this with the 'when in Rome' mentality and you have a recipe for licentiousness that even the Roman Empire would blush at.

> Expats take with them their personal values around sex and relationships when they go overseas.

Expats take with them their personal values around sex and relationships when they go overseas. Some of these values are culturally determined, or religiously determined within that culture, and have never been available as a freedom of choice like an expat arena posting often presents. In other words, no free choice was available as regards culturally acceptable behaviour surrounding sex and relationships at home. These values were a part of the cultural umbrella, as it were. Living under that particular umbrella determined behaviour. Living under a different cultural umbrella allows expats the freedom and the choice to behave differently with regard to sex and personal relationships should they choose to do so. Some expats take this as a free licence to explore, indulge and exploit all that is on offer. Couple this with an increased availability and opportunity and you have the basis of a sexual Nirvana of sorts.

Other expats, maybe from under the same home cultural umbrella or a different one, may have personalised their sexual and relationship values before they travel. People differ. People make choices for a variety of reasons. The difference between these two expat examples is visible in their behaviour. One set of expats will demonstrate sexual fidelity and commitment to a life-long partner irrespective of whatever cultural umbrella they live under. The other set of expats will often visibly change sexual behaviour with each differing cultural umbrella. These are choices people make. Local people notice what you do and how you live. Expats live in a global bubble. How could they not notice? Your sexual behaviour matters wherever you are in the world.

Building and sustaining a real relationship is easier between partners who hold similar values around sex and relationships particularly if both partners hold deep values around sexual fidelity and lifelong commitment. Couples who change values around sexuality with each different cultural umbrella will experience shifting sands underneath their feet. This model of living is more sustainable in the long term for men than for women. Older expat men are perceived as more attractive by local women in many cultures since they often have the power and money to assist success or a way out of poverty.

Cross-cultural relationships can, and do, work very well. There is the buzz of differentness, the language challenges, and the evolution from local to international. I believe these relationships call for deeper commitment and a dedication to continued leaning and adjustment as they have additional potential flashpoints around spending time with each international home base; equal access for grandparents to grandchildren; schooling choices; bilingualism; holidays, to name a few. As an international couple you will need more money to keep the extended family in touch and together.

Martin and I are from adjoining counties in Ireland. Less than 50km apart on the ground, the mindset is different. We were a mini cross-cultural couple from the beginning. "People over that way think different from us," my mother said. And she was right. Many of the big cross-cultural adjustments are mirrored in the small mini adjustments couples from different regions or cities within a single country experiences; or couples from different religions. The degrees of cultural adjustment range from minor to major. The one constant is change.

Both our children have international marriages, i.e. they are married to other nationals. But before they ever got to meet their life partners they themselves were experienced expats; they were more than their passport said they were. They see people first, culture second: the similarities, then any differences. And they know they can deal with cultural difficulties; they have done it before. These are key, identifiable expat traits I see time and again in successful international relationships around the world.

COMMUNICATION, or rather good communication, includes those essential skills of listening and speaking. For true understanding listening actively is equally as valuable as speaking with respectful candour. How you communicate will be determined partly by your personality and partly by the need you are experiencing to understand the other person and be understood in response. Better communication skills can be learned. Understanding cultural differences can be researched separately. Any expat worth his or her salt will have already invested time and effort researching the differences before leaving their home country anyway. When you get to your new country you will need to:

- Observe with your eyes and ears.
- Listen closely to what people say and how they say it.
- Respect local protocols.
- Ask questions if you do not understand. If it is not appropriate to ask at the time, ask later. Ask someone who knows, someone local you can trust. Another expat may not see the nuance you see.
- Beware of complacency. When you are complacent you will see your new country through your eyes only, interpreting events through your formative cultural understanding. This is when misunderstandings arise and if you are not aware of how they originated you will not be able to deal with them well. As an expat, you are always learning. Your new country may have similarities with your home country but it is not your home country. First and foremost, respect where you are.
- The nuances of deep, interpersonal spoken communication may be lost in the complexities of other language.

- The nuances of deep, interpersonal non-spoken communication may be lost in ignorance of acceptable cultural behaviour. Smiling is not regarded as friendly everywhere! And some women do not like to have the door held open for them. It denotes weakness in their culture.

WORK takes a huge chunk of time in an expat context. There are long days, late nights (in some professions), and weekends. The time-commitment factor is uncontested and inexorably linked to the package or deal a person is on. Most expats chase extra money in an overseas deal; some choose lifestyle. In the vast number of expat posts these two converge in some form or other; more money and the big villa; more money and the house at 'home'; more money and travel; more money and more possessions; more money and pay off bills. In this scenario it is unlikely that you will say to your boss that you need to spend more time with your partner, and sorry you cannot come to work today: it is decidedly more realistic to say to your partner that you need to spend more time at work, and sorry you will not be at home today. It is an uneven trade off. You sell your soul for a package while your lifetime commitment to your partner is put on hold, more holding, and more, until there is a real danger you will be enjoying the spoils of work on your own. This possible cost is rarely included in the equation. I say 'possible' because with awareness you can manage that beast called Expat Work to your advantage.

Work can add to the ease of making and developing personal relationships too. These can be between eligible singles, the married-available, and the locals. Going out to work perpetuates an alive-mindedness that can become deadened in at-home occupations. Going out to work demands a looking-good, taking-care-of-yourself dress code that is often abandoned for comfort clothing and a casual look for those home based individuals. Both of these at-work elements are attractive and the more time spent together can encourage a spark or blow a spark into a full blown flame. This is living and loving where you work, a canvas bursting with form and colour, while home can become a monochrome canvas with blurred edges and weeping forms.

Housing is an interesting element to consider in its effect on relationships. There is a tendency for big business to provide perceptually correct housing for its staff, particularly for its management, i.e. the bigger the employee the bigger the housing, and vice versa. Expensive housing can equate to 'remote and big' with cleaning staff and nannies, and - isolation. Staff can be housed for their employee status rather than for the way these employees want to live. Whatever housing option you choose will have limitations and can put strain on a relationship in the long term but perhaps the most intense of these is the 'alone in the big house' syndrome. It baffles me that erudite, smart people will not see that all the trimmings of expat wealth cannot replace loving, constant companionship. Many people tell me it is just short term, i.e. two years or three then it will all be back the way it was. No, it will not. You never step into the same river twice. Ask yourself honestly what is more important – work et al or your personal relationship or personal relationships plus children.

Staff crammed into small, noisy apartments will find it difficult to find that quiet romantic moment with a boyfriend/girlfriend. Some expats share apartments with other expats out of financial and loneliness considerations. When a romantic interest enters the scene it can be awkward. Expat staff living alone for prolonged periods may find it difficult to let anyone into their lives. Sometimes the disruption seems just too much especially if you never invite anyone into your inner living space. Couples in small apartments need time apart from each other or time alone in the apartment, some more than others. Decide on a routine where one party will leave for an hour on an errand or to have a coffee or a beer so the other can enjoy the peace and quiet of home alone.

Although this is not about personal relationships of the romantic kind I use it here for illustration purposes.

My daughter and I shared a small apartment in Shimokitizawa, Tokyo for a year. We also worked for the same school but in different departments but it did mean we could enjoy going to work in the morning together as well as coming home together in the evening. Our year together remains a special memory, a year in my daughter's adult life I was honoured to share.

There were days we would walk all the way home together; days we would wander the shops; days when we would share cooking. But there were days when we needed space and we quickly decided on being honest with each other. It wasn't that we disliked each other or had an argument. We just needed personal recharge time from the work day. Between the train station and home was a small coffee shop we would frequent together and singularly. We quickly came to joke, 'your turn or mine?' as we passed it. It added the silence around our lives that we needed at that moment. It facilitated a discharge of grumpiness and negativity from the day and enriched our subsequent 'clean' time together.

Do not be afraid to discuss the need for 'alone' time in a shared living space. This is not the same as going home to your shared apartment and spending the evening in your room. Many of you will have discipline memories around spending time in your room so creating a living environment like this will emphasise the negativity, the need to escape, which can become equated with a choking relationship, one that needs to be escaped from when in reality what needs to happen is time-out to enjoy your living space alone.

NON-WORK is a challenge of a different magnitude when it comes to personal relationships. Often the person going out to work would love to stay at home and the person at home visualises work as exciting, the escape from the mundane or the aloneness, or just to escape the children for a while! Many difficulties arise from the legal inability of the non-work person to use his or her talents and skills to contribute in a worthwhile way to the community and/or their bank account. In this new country they have no separate identity; they are here as an adjunct to their working partner, their sole purpose in life to support him or her in their job. What the non-worker wants or can provide has no meaning apart from their worker partner. It is easy to slide into invisibility and depression. But then, thankfully, there are only so many reruns of CSI that can be watched without going insane! It really is a sink or swim situation trailing spouses and partners find themselves in. Any one single person who has survived the process is an immensely resourceful, proactive, and independent individual capable of tackling any problem life throws at them. And that's just those who survive! Think what those who thrive can do!

RELATIONSHIPS are challenging to get right at any time, in any location, but in an expat situation there are particular issues that can cause havoc if not managed adroitly.

• Long working hours. The vast majority of expats work excessively long hours when on an overseas posting. This is often glossed over because the package is so good or you are so excited about living overseas you will do almost anything for the experience. For many, this work can involve a lot of travel inside the country or region; sometimes worldwide. Will this work for you? Can you sustain a serious, long-term relationship living and working like this? Unless you are working too, as a trailing spouse you will spend the vast majority of your days alone. What will you do? How will you gainfully fill them? Or will you play the blame game – blaming your partner for your inability to move forward?

• Managing additional discretionary income. The big three options are: spend it; save it; or pay the outstanding bills first. What you choose to do will be in keeping with your values in life and your mental attitude surrounding this particular expat post. It is not unusual for one person to want to spend some of the hard-earned cash on exploring their new surroundings a bit; having a better lifestyle; and acquiring some big-ticket items they have always dreamed of while the other wishes to clear debt and invest in something back 'home'. Do you have agreed protocols around money-management? If you are a trailing spouse/partner, how will you deal with managing the joint money only one of you is earning? As the earner, how do you visualise your partner using this money? Is there a cultural difference between the way money is handled in permanent relationships in your culture and that of your partner?

• Physical isolation. It is possible to be physically isolated in the centre of a 25 million city just as well as living on a small island with a population of 1000. As an expat, you live the fish-bowl life. You are different. You are exotic. You represent something different to the society you are living in. You are dangerous. You do not automatically fit in. You will remain at arms-length from the local people until you make the effort to integrate. Your partner may be all you will have in this move to relate to beyond the superficial level. Make sure you are there for each other. It can be really difficult for the working partner to have energy at the end of the day for the trailing partner. It can be really difficult for the trailing partner to not pick a fight if their working partner continuously comes home late and exhausted. Physical presence is not enough to keep the relationship alive. There needs to be meaningful interaction on a regular basis. Sadly, most expats work exhaustively in their expat posting and 'live' during the short holidays. It takes strong commitment for a relationship to survive this. Alternatively you may have started a new relationship here. Is this because you were thrown together? Have you thought about your continuing relationship in a different expat context? Is your partner a local? Will she/he leave with you at the end of your contract? Are you happy to stay forever? Do you know if your local partner will be allowed to leave with you? Do you know if you will be allowed to stay beyond your contract? Will your local partner be able to travel with you on other expat postings, i.e., will other countries give him/her a visa?

• Gender segregation. Expats moving from a free, equal society into one of gender segregation will find differing challenges and new ways of living depending on which side of the gender divide they belong to. Public heterosexual contact between singles alone may be frowned upon, curtailed, and maybe even earn the perpetrators a custodial sentence, a public flogging, and/or expulsion from the country. Gay and lesbian relationships are also non rigour. Everything public about relationships will need to be reviewed in detail. Legally, only spouses will be admitted into the country with the work partner. Society, not your personal relationship and values, will determine behaviour in such a society. It is not for the faint-hearted. Often it is where 'good' money can be made; and this draw can overshadow the difficulties ahead. If you are a single woman looking for a date, look within the expat community. If you are a man looking for a date, look within the expat community. Discretion is the name of the game.

• Beware! Predator alert! There was a time when someone would read 'predator' and the only gender to fit the bill would be male. While this remains mostly so in the expat context it is fair to say women have moved the goalposts on this but in two specific ways mainly – climbing the career ladder, and escaping their home culture. For men, it is more about conquest and sex. Expat men hold a fascination for foreign women, the older the better because they are more likely to have the power and the money to change lives. Some expat men prey on this fascination leaving a trail of destruction in their wake, and I do not just mean single men. Some expat men prey on local women only; other expat men, any female in sight. Local women who prey on expat men are more directed. They choose carefully. They want up or out, or both. Luckily, the predatory percentage in any expat posting remains low. Most expats and locals alike are mature, lovely people who respect each other and behave respectfully towards each other. Sometimes it is hard to avoid the destruction a predatory encounter provides. Loneliness is a hard part of expat living and who does not want a close, loving relationship however long the odds. Alcohol can grease the slope too and many lonely expats drink beyond moderation to get through tough times alone, and there are always those tough times in any posting. Beware though: a personal predatory encounter is always compromising even if not totally destructive.

- To stray or not to stray. There are so many opportunities to stray into and out of relationships in expat postings, and there is always someone willing to provide for your deepest needs. Some male expats bypass this minefield by opting to visit a brothel regularly even though they will be expelled from the country if found out. Expat women do not have this escape route: it is personal relationships or nothing. Lonely people are vulnerable people. Long working hours creates possibilities away from home or a loved one. Exciting work colleagues relieves routine. But not everyone wants a quick fix. Most men and women respect permanence in relationships; they desire enduring and trusting relationships. And they will wait for the right person or wait with the right person. Expat postings test even the strongest of relationships. What will you do if you are a trailing spouse and your partner strays? What will you do if you are in a new relationship and your partner strays? Is it all just an opportunistic mistake? Does it really mean nothing?

- Sex anyone? If sex is what you want, it is not difficult to find as an expat. Rules seem different in an expat posting and many people will look at sexual behaviour differently in a different environment particularly if the norms around sexual behaviour are more 'free' in the new environment, or appear so to a transient expat. Many foreign countries do not care what expats do to/with expats but they are deeply concerned about what expats do to/with their people. But there is a strong curiosity element: locals want to know if foreigners really have the same parts as local men and women; expats want to know how locals will behave in bed. Most expat men are non-discriminatory: they will bed local and other expat women alike as long as availability and opportunity coincide. Most local men are picky: they make a distinction between how a local woman will serve their needs and how they will have to perform to meet the needs of an expat woman. If an expat woman wants to have a relationship of substance in an expat posting, whether local or expat, she will have to be prepared to wait. It does happen. But the longer she waits, the harder it is to share her personal space with a meaningful 'other'.

- Anonymity illusion. It is easy to pretend that what you get up to as an expat in your personal life is private. It is no one else's business but yours. After all, that is what happens at home, right? Maybe. Maybe not. But this saying that 'what happens in Rome, stays in Rome' is an illusion. If no one else knows how you have behaved, maybe even strayed, you do; and it then depends if your behaviour has been congruent or incongruent with your personal values as to how your actions affect your life. And there is ALWAYS someone else who knows what has happened – the other person or persons involved. Expat communities tend to be small even if just in comparison to the total population numbers. There is always someone who sees what is going on or observes some inexplicable fallout around you. And there is nothing juicier than a snippet of indiscretion or the fall from grace of a pillar of society. Maybe that pillar will not fall if he or she is prepared to compromise their personal reputation for the sake of their professional one? Maybe you care about your reputation; maybe you do not. But remember – you live in a fishbowl. It suddenly becomes a very small world indeed.

- Revenge. If you have got to the stage where you will indulge in sexual promiscuity to get revenge on a loved partner you are in trouble wherever you live. Your values are screwed. Something is just plain wrong – and two wrongs do not make a right. Sometimes expat living can mess with your head and you can end up making choices that just do not make sense. But what makes sense is that people hurt each other by their behaviour; that is not new. It is not even environment dependent. It can happen anywhere in the world. But if it happens halfway around the world, chances are you do not have the close support network you would have back home if this happened there. And if you are fully dependent on the offender, you are skating on thin ice. You may well wallow in misery on the first supportive shoulder offered. Who can blame you? At least someone is there for you, are they not? Revenge can quickly morph into a very different uncontrollable beast. Have you got the fare home?

These issues exist whether you arrive at your expat post as a married couple, heterosexual partners, same-sex partners, single, young or old. They exist for the partner who decides to stay in their home country too.

MARRIED COUPLES: For any couple working overseas, the secret to having a successful relationship is in the details. The details are very simple, common principles based on core values. These are:

- Respect
- Commitment
- Communication
- Caring

What I often hear instead is:

- Opportunity
- Excitement
- Activity
- Desire

There is no reason why the second set should not exist; after all, that is often why people live the expat life. Problems arise though when it usurps the first set which sits at the core of a relationship.

'Opportunity' can become 'opportunity at anything'; 'activity' or its more obvious cousin, 'hectivity', can leave few moments of quiet reflection together; in fact, there is a real danger of the quiet reflective times together becoming boring as the adrenalin rush demands more each time for the same high. The drive to see all there is to see; to meet with everyone and anyone lest any be offended; to put in as much as possible into every day because we will not be here forever, etc. may well prove too much. It is possible that one or other partner may find the local men or women alluring, exotic, and desirable and begin comparing them with their partner. If both partners are employed their working teams may provide an exciting challenge for the mind and eye. Or they may be the very opposite, sending you scurrying home to the loving arms of your partner. You may find you have choices around individuals you meet that will test your relationship with your partner, your commitment to your relationship. Expect these elements to arise. Your response will determine your future.

STAY AT HOME PARTNER: If you are a stay-at-home partner through choice or because you cannot legally work:
- Keep looking good.
- Spend money on yourself.
- Keep healthy.
- Keep fit.
- Use your 'free' time wisely. Build for the future.
- Remember why you are both here. Move on.
- Stay with your working partner. Remaining in your home country while your partner works away from home for long periods is a disaster waiting to happen.

WORKING PARTNER: If you are the working partner:
- Prioritise your personal relationship.

- Stick to your 'together' time.
- Compliment your partner.
- Never compare your partner to someone at work (or anyone else for that matter).
- Help around the house.
- Gift generously.
- Empower your partner.
- Delegate.

SINGLE WOMEN: If you are a single woman:
- Recognise that looking for a date is a healthy thing.
- Review your values around relationships, and particularly sex.
- Review what values you are looking for in a potential date/partner.
- Recognise and understand the cultural norms which exist where you now are.
- Be clear about the depth of your desire for a potential mate/partner.
- If you need to reverse-locate to fulfil a biological drive, plan to do so. Be honest with yourself. There are far too many unhappy 40 something women out there who have not faced down this dilemma.
- If you are looking for a sex friend only make this clear to your date. Contrary to popular opinion, men may be looking for depth and continuity in their relationships, and they can be hurt just as easily as women when things fall apart.

SINGLE MEN: If you are a single man:
- Be clear about what you want in a potential relationship.
- Communicate this openly and clearly to your date.
- Practice safe sex for everybody's sake.

- Keep what happens in the bedroom, in the bedroom.
- Recognise and respect the cultural norms.
- Review your values. Are you going to change your sexual behaviour simply because you are in a different country? The opportunity presents itself?
- Think responsibly around relationships. What may be understood as normal practice back home may be seen differently here.
- Think long term too. Can you manage an international family?

SAME SEX PARTNERS: If you are looking for a same sex partner:
- Be clear about what you want in a relationship.
- Review your values around same sex relationships.
- What happens in the bedroom stays in the bedroom.
- Know the cultural norms in your new country.
- Plan your expat life carefully to provide the best opportunity for happiness.
- Be sensitive to your partner about coming out. It is worth waiting until you are both in synch on this.

DISTANCE RELATIONSHIPS: If you are involved in a distance relationship:
- They can work really well.
- They take the same commitment as a face-to-face relationship.
- Friends and family may be sceptical that you really are in a relationship.
- Friends may try and set you up with dates.
- Distance relationships involve Skype calls at key social times or middle of the night.
- They involve more travel and lots of tearful goodbyes.

- Ultimately they involve movement. One of you has to move towards the other or you both move to a neutral, new venue.

Ultimately you will need to get to know each other all over again in your new 'always together' environment.

18

AND BEGGARS EVERYWHERE

I HAVE ENCOUNTERED beggars in all my expat postings, and in my home capital too. Whether they appeal to my emotions in desperation or target my emotions mercilessly I am stricken inside because I cannot fulfil their desires; I cannot lift them from their poverty of body, mind or spirit alone. And there is my first mistake – I transfer my view of life onto each and every one of them. I respect each for the person he or she is and want something better for them. But for some, what they are doing now is better! And who am I to judge? Their dream may be reduced to the next bite of food. And yet I hold back because if I give this one money within seconds she will be joined by another and another dashing from the doorways and alleys where they have been lurking, observing. I am now concerned for my safety and that of the one I have given money too as I see her surrounded by a hungry mob. I wind up the window and am driven away in tears. Have I done more harm than good here today?

Expats are a soft touch for beggars for a variety of reasons. We are highly visible; we stand out, usually. And we are generous because we earn more money, usually. We should be giving back to our new society, right? We will never miss the odd coin or two, right? And beggars know how the locals will respond to them: they have worked that out a long time ago. To the vast majority, they are a nuisance to be scorned, ignored or chased away. But who are these beggars anyway? They may be:

- Disenfranchised citizens moved by their government from their land/home for a variety of reasons and end up as migrants in the large cities without any legal status.
- Long term refugees who have not been given any legal status so they cannot work to support themselves.
- Gypsies who choose to travel widely whose traditional crafts are no longer in demand by a growing, sophisticated, technological society.
- Genuinely poor people who have no access to education or health services or work.
- Elderly people who have nowhere to go.
- Drug addicts
- Alcoholics.
- Citizens with mental problems.
- Abused individuals escaping their terror.
- Handicapped people.
- 'Slave' members of an organised begging gang pimped by ruthless leaders.
- Or any segment of society shunned by the greater body of people because of a real or perceived threat, e.g., Ebola orphans; leprosy sufferers; AIDs patients; or just because someone is different.

And as my mother used to say – 'There go I but for the grace of God'.

They may be:

- Old men
- Old women
- Young females with babies
- Young disfigured men
- Children of all ages
- Orphans

I was walking down Hong Mei Lu a few days after arriving in Shanghai when I first saw her. She was curled up on the steps of Starbucks, a tiny figure of a woman, light enough for a faint breeze to blow her away. Her face was a rough terrain of deep lines; her nails dirty and chipped. But it was her gentle demeanour on looking into her deep brown eyes that captivated me. My heart contracted. I was looking at an eighty year old version of my own mother transported across the world. What had she done in life to deserve ending up begging on the streets of Shanghai?

She was on the street every day and I made sure to seek her out and try and slip her a few RMB on the sly while dropping some into her plastic cup. She was being monitored by a mean bandana man further down the street. At best, all we could do was smile at each other. She was a migrant, displaced from her home in the national drive for commercialism. She started to avoid me or covered her cup when she saw me, turning away if her mentor was about. Her 'friends' included a lovely young man who crept up and down the street every day on a skateboard, his gloved hands his only way of propulsion and protection against the dirty street he called home, his lower, wasted body crushed under his torso; and another young man whose tortured wrists could have been the result of deliberate misplacement so he could fare better in his begging.

I was walking towards my lovely old lady one day. She had her back to me, her cup help hopefully outwards to an upwardly mobile young local man stepping towards Starbucks, the ubiquitous cigarette dangling from his mouth. Without breaking stride as he came alongside her, he drew the cigarette from his mouth and quenched it in her cup before skipping up the steps for his brew. She was visibly shocked before slumping to the ground to rescue her few pennies before the cup melted. There is no dignity in being poor.

Beggars everywhere have issues and problems in their background a few of which are listed here:

- Literacy
- Birth status
- Residency
- Handicaps
- Personal vulnerabilities
- Self-confidence
- Learning abilities
- Family support
- Health care

> **Beggars are people-smart because they have to be to survive.**

A great number would rather not be on the streets, ever. Others are now doing well on the streets and do not want to change. They have found a way to survive, maybe even thrive. It may be the only way for them. They begin to build a life around their begging. It has become a job. The begging they had started in desperation they have now become dependent on. They see no way out. They must work it until they reach a 'comfortable state', whatever that means. One beggar in Shanghai worked the train stations seventeen hours a day, every day. He was a migrant to the city with no papers. His goal was to make enough money to pay for his young daughter to go to school. With no family papers she was not entitled to schooling in Shanghai. He was determined to break the poverty cycle he had been dumped into.

Beggars are people-smart because they have to be to survive. They are top profilers. Their survival depends on it. They read people well. They know about concealment; how to disappear quickly; how to escape from authority. They exploit the public through emotional blackmail. Do they even see whom they are targeting? Maybe. Maybe not. I guess it just depends.

I was standing outside Novy Smichov waiting for the tram. It was lunchtime and busy. From my right I could hear her coming, a Roma lady, begging. The Czech's don't like Gypsies/Roma. There is a long history of Gypsy/Roma travel in central Europe that the settled have issues with. She was ignored all the way down the line but she kept going. She arrived at me and delivered the same speech. When I didn't respond she moved on to my right. Coincidently I moved likewise to meet a friend further down. She came towards me again, same speech, same drill. When she stood in front of me for the second time delivering her speech I realised she didn't recognise me; she hadn't even seen me the first time. She was completely disassociated from her begging. Did she really hate it so much, I wondered? Then I felt really guilty I hadn't given her the loose change I had in my pocket because I bet she really needed it.

I have watched expats and locals alike in their interactions with beggars. Some are more expressive in their emotions than others. The main ones represented are:

- Pity
- Concern
- Fear
- Disgust

- Revulsion
- Anger
- Indifference

What I hear from expats is how much they dislike being HAD, being played by beggars. Add to that being: followed, touched, pulled at, shouted at and made to run a gauntlet of emotions by skilful emotional blackmailers and it is easy to see how many give up and never give out a penny ever again.

There is no dignity in being poor. And there is no dignity in being HAD either.

Beggars want the same currency you and I do; they want money. I see people giving food, clothing from their own backs, and offers of help. But beggars do not eat the same food as you or I. They do not wear clothes like you and I. In their circles, our money goes further. First and foremost your decision is to give or not; then additionally what to give. Interacting with beggars on the street demands an individual response. It is always an emotive encounter. You choose what you do and move on. There are charities that seek to help on a macro level; a place where you can donate in anonymity; a sanitised experience that assuages your need to give while delegating the front line work to those who are willing and trained to do so. These charities are entirely necessary as not everyone has the necessary empathy and temperament to deal respectfully, in an informed manner, with these disenfranchised individuals. Beggars are individuals with a personal story like you and me. The uniformity of their survival needs often blind us to the individual tragedy begging before us.

I love Christmas in Prague for a variety of reasons: the atmosphere at the market stalls; the steam from my mulled wine rising into the frigid air; and being with family, most of all that. It is always special being with my family.

We walk on the Charles Bridge in the morning, the packed snow crunching under our feet. He is kneeling on the bridge, his cap on the ground before him, his dog lying on the dirty blanket, breathing easily. The smell of drink is overwhelming. The man has no jacket. How can he not be hypothermic? Our son rushes forward and taking off his jacket wraps it around the man, and then grabs my scarf and cap to add to his comfort. But the man only looks with glazed, uncomprehending eyes at the still-empty cap in front of him. He does not move a muscle as we cut short our walk and hurry back to the warmth of the car.

It is an on-going conundrum: to give what we see as necessary or to give what the individual begging before us sees as necessary in that moment. We live by different lights. Maybe that beggar on the Charles Bridge wanted money to buy food for his dog. After all, it was the dog that was on the blanket while he knelt on the snowy ground.

To give or not to give; to help or not to help; to see or not to see: the choice remains with you.

19

EPILOGUE: SOCIAL LIVING

THE LOSS OF meaningful personal contact is inevitable in a move abroad even if you are travelling with a significant other. In your new life they will not be as available to you as they are now; or they will be available to you in a new way that you both have to make sense of. The same is true for accompanying family. Children are just as much adrift as you are. Non-accompanying children muddle by until they learn to cope as self-reliant individuals.

I arrived in the UK a little naïve. In an English speaking environment I expected to make friends easily. I make friends easily. I am interested in people; their lives and their aspirations. I was looking forward to a break too, a time just for me until the children were settled and I could look to my own career. We had planned that this would be my opportunity too; time to develop my career in contrast to a money job. I expected to carry on as I left off at home. But I fell afoul of a very common mistake people make in emigrating to a similar language culture: I saw the language similarities and failed to see the culture differences. And – we had a home for my husband's job which left me physically isolated until I got my own car. It was great after that but initially it didn't suit my needs at all.

In the beginning it didn't really matter what language was spoken around me. I knew no one. Not one single person. And, as is usual, my husband was working, or reading up about work procedures and processes, 24/7 in his new job. This pattern is commonplace; it repeated itself many times in our moves around the world. But back then, I was confounded by what I was experiencing. One week passed. Two weeks passed. This seemed like a lifetime isolation sentence! Then Mary came to my rescue and life began to balance again.

I have had many different friends in my journeys: survival friends; friends I am comfortable with at different levels; true friends I can trust with my ongoing struggles and challenges; and best friends I can share my life with. The only thing that makes these different is the environment element because many of these are other nationals, people I would normally have no contact with whatsoever apart from my expat life. And, after separating, this element means we either never see each other again or we work at making the distance friendship last in the hope that our paths will cross again in the future. Many I will keep in occasional email contact with; some will drift away from me instantly. The shutters will come down so suddenly it is shocking. I believe that this can be because that friend had more invested in me for their personal survival than I had reckoned with or I was truly an opportunistic part of their network and I would be discarded anyway as soon as I became less useful. It is frightening to review these friendships and realise how much an occasional part of the patchwork of their lives I was, an element discarded as effortlessly as the wrapper from a chocolate bar. I call this way of living Surface Living and if you want to check this out for yourself, look around you and see all the slightly drunk, or more so, individuals who are experiencing problems in their personal life or are single with loneliness pouring out of every pore. Reality is a fickle thing, and they have lost touch with it and with their own selves. Their reinvention of themselves in this new place is not congruent with their deeper needs. I am fortunate to have a necklace of friends around the world that I respect and admire. They anchor me in my life journeys; encourage me with their wisdom and expertise; and support me with their unfailing love.

My personal relationships with the significant others in my life, my husband and children, were tough to maintain and progress because of two factors: busyness and distance. I often felt a work widow: even though I worked full time myself I would be home most days before my husband. By the time of my trailing spouse posting in Shanghai we had worked through some issues around the tyranny of work that meant we had regular quality time together. It is up to each couple to manage this for themselves but believe me, work widows or widowers are not happy people. I found it difficult to share my husband all the time. I began to doubt his commitment to me. He was always irritated at my bringing up the subject. I'm glad we had some 'miles in the tyres' of our marriage before we left. It's been wonderful to realise that at our core we remain the same. That which attracted us to each other is still there after we assimilated so many other cultures into our lives together. Adjustment to circumstances is the name of the game. Adjustment to circumstances and a significant other is the name of the game for those who meet abroad. It's an exciting double whammy. Is the expat abroad the same as the person in their home culture? I believe the expat abroad is more true to themselves than the person at home. So have no fear if you meet your loved one abroad. You have met the real person outside the social umbrella that can force conformity because what would the neighbour's say!

I cannot tell you how much I missed my children's friendship and love on tap at home. And I know the feelings are mutual. They told me. How lovely is that! I am so grateful for modern technology that keeps us in touch but digital hugs just aren't the same. Distance happens in families anyway as children grow up and realise their own trajectory through life. Expat living expedites the process, changing the timeline as well as offering that glimpse around the corner at possible alternative lifestyles. But your children are always your children; you are always a parent. The additional joy is possibly becoming friends and sharing life in such a special way.

I am a kind hearted person and people begging to live break my heart. From a seemingly accident of birth, I am here and they are destitute. I earn a good salary, an expat salary, which is greater than even the locals I work with. It has to be. I have more overheads. But these people have nothing for whatever reason. And it is hard to fathom the reason. And I realise I just can't. There are as many reasons as people. I do not have one way I respond to these people, many elderly and many children. I give to charities, I put money in their cup, I say, 'Not today, thank you.' I walk around the block to avoid them when I have helped them for a few days in a row. I avoid eye contact with the man in the bandana who has his 'team' on the street. He is a mean one. We parted company for good one day after he clung to my arm and wouldn't let go. I never gave to him after that and he would just laugh at me as I shook my head at him and said no. I had adapted and he moved onto new expats, always expats.

My most sad experience was in Lagos with children begging. They banged on the car window for as long as we were stopped in traffic. We gave to one on one occasion to see him surrounded by a gang of others as we drove away. We feared for his safety. And that was another generation on the streets if they lived that long. My most fearful experience was also in Lagos. One Sunday morning we were pulled over by the 'Yellow Peril', a group of policemen so called because of their uniform and actions. Apparently our front tyres had protruded a fraction over the line at the lights and one descended on us gleefully. Any excuse to stop the white man and make some money. He was followed by four others, from where, we didn't see.

They piled into the back seat and threatened us with prison for our offense if we didn't 'dash' or bribe them. We had often been stopped at this crossing. We would simply be asked for the price of a breakfast which we didn't mind as we were aware that these people were often not paid by the government for months. But this was different. Here were five opportunistic big guys demanding money. We were lucky they weren't armed. It was not begging as we understand it in the western world; this was begging with menace. If going to the airport would not be a perilous journey without our Nigerian driver, I would have turned the car and left there and then; I'd had enough.

Expat living is not for the faint hearted. It is an uphill struggle despite the excitement but it is so very well worth it. I have learned so much about who I am really; I have become a survivor in another land; inside, I am becoming a global citizen.

'These men are my friends: he that loves me, he that hates me, and he that is indifferent to me. Who loves me teaches me tenderness. Who hates me teaches me caution. Who is indifferent to me teaches me self-reliance.'

J. E. Dinger

PART 4
HOW AM I DOING

"If you live long enough you'll make mistakes. But if you learn from them, you'll be a better person. It's how you handle adversity, not how it affects you. The main thing is never quit, never quit, never quit."

William J Clinton

20

PROLOGUE: HOW AM I DOING

BEFORE LONG, IN your new post, you will begin to ask yourself how you are doing. Is this working for you? Is it what you expected? You will begin to moderate your expectations in relation to your personal experience on the ground. And so you should. Your contract is likely to be a finite one and you will need to get the best out of it while contributing equally to your environment. You may find you are giving more than you expected; giving differently than you expected; or that you feel differently around your posting than you expected. Maybe a colleague is challenging you in ways you find difficult to manage; maybe your boss is delegating too much; or maybe the money is not covering all you hoped for in this short contract timeframe. Maybe your family is unhappy, unfulfilled, or downright miserable. So many maybes yet expats are adept at skirting the issues, putting the discomfort down to not having adjusted yet. How long should you wait to review your situation? And what signs should you be looking out for anyway? Where to begin!

Begin with your **WORLD**:
Work
Ourselves

Rest and relaxation
Life and living
Dreams

Ideally we would all love these to be in balance continuously but that is rarely so. We find the elements intertwined with one taking centre stage, work. Expat living can sometimes seem all about work, especially if you choose to live and work in an immersive work environment like Singapore, for example, everything else taking a lesser place. When expat work becomes the expat life then every other element of living is experienced only through that expat work. And the location of that expat work, and the people that inhabit the workplace, become your new local village. Personal decisions will be made in reference to work. The roster becomes the rulebook; the person lost in the worker. This is commonplace initially. If it progresses past six months you can become stuck in the familiar. It is also commonplace that while things are going well there will seem no need for review. But the minute the negatives come at you your subconscious will prompt you to review. And you will review against a previously better situation or a dream you held for this post.

Part 4 explores the way thinking can cloud our judgement or clarify our reality. The language we use in everyday conversation can shed light on our thought processes. Listen to what you are saying. Identify your negative or positive way of thinking around the situation you are focusing on. Consciously changing your thinking can change your life.

"Whether you think you can or whether you think you can't, you're probably right."
Henry Ford

21

EARNING A LIVING OR LIVING A LIFE

IT IS VERY common to speak about earning a living in going abroad to work as an expat. That is what most expats are doing. They are grasping the opportunity to accelerate their living experience outside the home normal. It is a personal choice. But wherever you are working you are living also. Living is not just for the holidays or when you retire. The quality of that living experience is only partly dependent on the living earned through work. What makes a huge difference is how we perceive the move is working out; how much we value personal freedom in relation to money spent and money saved; our choices around fulfilment in relationships; and our plans for the future, to name a few. The ideal way is to live a life while earning a living, something I believe everyone can achieve.

> Earning a living is a necessity while living a life is the icing on the cake, the rewards of earning a living, and where most personal choice presents.

Earning a living can be motivation at any age or career stage to live the expat life. So can living a life. We hear the phrase 'earning a living' often enough for it to be commonplace. Living a life is almost considered above your station; something that will get you into trouble; in the realms of irresponsible behaviour. Each present differing characteristics.

Characteristics of earning a living can include:
- Work focus for life or the long haul
- Steady
- Slow pace of living
- Money job
- Singularity of work experience with promotion from within
- Repetitive
- Regular routine
- Regular work hours
- Pay covers expenses and some additional elements
- Localised
- Limited choice

Characteristics of living a life can include:
- New experiences
- Promotion outside the local environment
- Risk taking
- High pace of living
- High elements of choice
- Career progression
- Seek opportunities
- Interrupted routines
- Intense working timetable
- High salary plus benefits
- Travel
- Freedom

There are distinct differences in the language associated with the phrases 'Earning a living' and 'Living a life' which correlate with the above characteristics. I have illustrated some of these in the following Figures 1 and 2. These are used unconsciously and can offer you an insight into how you are thinking around your work and living move. They can also offer your employer, supervisor, and colleague the same insight into how you are thinking about work. And they can also offer you insight into how these same people are approaching work too. The good news is that once you are aware of these you get to choose which way you want to approach your working and living from now on. By choosing how you think around any issue, problem or event will change your approach, and change will follow. But you may not want change; you may be completely happy with the status quo. Change will move you out of your comfort zone. The choice to listen to how you think is yours. The choice to change how you think is yours.

Figure 4: Earning a living

Earning a living is a necessity while living a life is the icing on the cake, the rewards of earning a living, and where most personal choice presents. Additionally not everyone has the same perception of what living a life means while most everyone knows the reality of earning a living. In the end how you earn a living and enjoy living a life is a choice. Sometimes the choices are limited locally; sometimes globally. The expat is often perceived as chasing money so he can have his cake and eat it in record time while the non-expat is often perceived as the backbone of the country, the safe, dependable worker who will grow business margins and enjoy her pension in retirement.

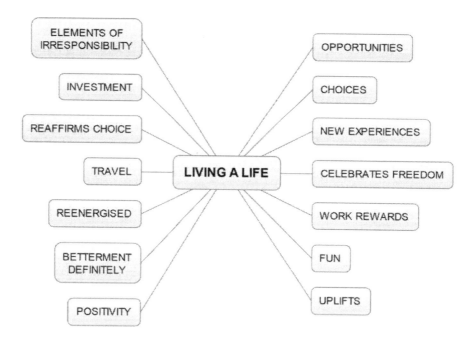

Figure 5: Living a life

Life balance is important whether you are earning a living or living a life. For the expat this has the added challenge of immediacy. You are here in this amazing country for a set period of time and you want to enjoy the environment as well as work. From the start, routines are interrupted and you will need to seek a balance in the important areas of work, family, relationships, health, finances, travel, and self development. Work has a way of looking after itself. The main way you will need to balance this is managing your discretionary work hours so you are not working 24/7 although this can, and does, happen in short burst work commitments. There is a tendency for expats to over commit because of the good deal they are on and not take care of their health or relationships. The work may be exciting and stimulating, and the finances stacking up positively but there is little time for anything else in your life. In this common scenario, before long, diminishing returns will set in through tiredness or exhaustion, mental capacity will decline, and health problems will begin to present themselves.

Check out your life balance right now. Follow Figure 6 on the next page for example:

- Draw a big circle
- Draw diagonals from the centre to the circumference for the areas you want to include in your life. Start with radials for Work, Family/Relationships, Health, Finance, Travel, and Self Development. You can develop this personally later. The size of the segments created is unimportant. The focus is on the radial.
- On each radial, measure off in equal increments from 0 at the centre to 10 at the circumference.
- Mark where you think you are along each radial, 0 being low satisfaction, 10 being total satisfaction.
- When you have done this for each radial/life element, join the dots. Ideally, what you are looking for is a smooth inside circle indicating all important areas of your life are in synchronous balance. Usually what people find is that one or two areas are much closer to 0 or 10 than they realised. These are the priority areas to bring back into balance.

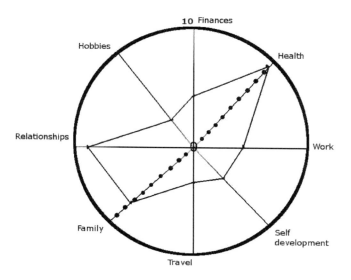

Figure 6: Life Balance Wheel originally created by Paul J. Meyer, founder of the Success Motivation® Institute, Inc. The Wheel of Life® is registered by www.mindtools.com where you can find more information on its use and application.

Language matters every second of every day. What we hear ourselves say, what we hear others say, and the self chatter that goes on incessantly in our minds matter. We can learn a great deal by just listening; we can learn a great deal more by understanding the nuances of what we hear. What we hear ourselves say has a huge impact on our emotional perceptions around work and life. And since we make our decisions at gut level these emotional perceptions sing a very loud tune indeed. We often struggle with being logical around decisions because of our emotional perceptions. But, good news, we can learn to identify when we are trailing into emotional perception territory just by listening to the words we choose to describe life events.

Here are two review exercises to get you started:

Review 1: What language are you using?

- ☐ Listen to the words you use to describe work
- ☐ Write down habitual phrases or exclamations
- ☐ At the end of the day what words do you use to describe your experience
- ☐ How are you feeling about getting up for work in the morning
- ☐ How do you feel at the end of the day
- ☐ How was your weekend
- ☐ Can you recognise a colleague who is earning a living
- ☐ Can you recognise a colleague who is living a life
- ☐ What do these colleagues have in common with you
- ☐ What do you have in common with these colleagues
- ☐ Do you favour one set of companionship over another
- ☐ Are you mostly reactive in work
- ☐ Is it all about you
- ☐ Is it all about someone else

Review 2: What language can you change?

- ☐ What language choices would you like to make
- ☐ Do you believe you have a choice
- ☐ Are you free to articulate new ways of thinking
- ☐ What will you lose if you do
- ☐ What will you gain if you do
- ☐ Is it too much trouble to be bothered with any of this

☐ Are the changes too small for the predicament you find yourself in now

☐ Are you too comfortable with the status quo to change anything

Wherever you are on the pay scale only you get to determine how you think in your own mind. You can be in a restrictive money job and be the happiest person on the planet or you can be miserable and stressed. Alternatively you can have your dream career and be stretched to the limits of your capabilities so you have no time to enjoy the rich rewards of your labour. More may need to be considered than changing how you think around a situation to move into a better place but changing how you think is a first step anyone can take anywhere. It puts you back in control of your life. You become identified with the choices you make and others will begin to relate to you differently because you ARE different. Chances are you will find issues and problems resolve themselves or at least you are proactive in the process rather than being continuously reactive.

Some examples of proactive versus reactive thinking are:

Event or occasion	Proactive thinking	Reactive thinking
You are asked to cover someone else's shift	You see this as an opportunity to work in a different area; to be upskilled; or to earn extra money. There may be something in it for you down the line.	You do not see how you can do this extra work in an unfamiliar area. How could your boss/supervisor ask you to do this! Don't they know you're super busy already.
An event at work didn't	You are	You are not to blame

go the way you expected it to and you have to report in.	disappointed but now you have more information around the issue than before and you have a new solution that will serve all better in the long run.	for how it worked out. Your colleague screwed up or the technology let you down. It's not your fault.
All staff are required to partake in training.	You are excited about learning something new. You see this as a stepping stone to career improvement within the firm.	You are annoyed you have to go through this again! You can do your job perfectly well without having to spend a whole day listening to someone telling you what you can or cannot do.
You are offered a promotion outside your current area at work.	This is a bit daunting at first but you will be fully trained in the new area. It's a chance to show you are a team player, and it will enhance your CV for the future.	This is not something you are in the least interested in. You can think of a hundred reasons why this will not suit you. But you might just consider it in case a colleague you don't like gets in before you.
You come home from work and your partner/roommate asks how your day was.	You reply it was busy good. There were a few awkward customers but it all worked out in the	You had a shit day. Everyone dumped on you. You had too much to do, as usual, and nobody noticed

	end	that.
You are out for a meal with your partner, colleagues or friends. They don't have what you like on the Menu.	You are disappointed but you're up for trying something else in its place. Who knows, you might like it better. And you don't want to spoil the evening by being selfish. It's only a meal out after all.	Just your luck! They must have known you were coming. You suggest going somewhere else where you can have what you want. Your whole world feels threatened.
You are reviewing your current work and living position.	All things taken in balance, it is good. You decide you need to look at two areas in particular and review how you feel about them in a month or so.	Depending on your mood, everything is crap or everything is great. You let singular events represent the whole of your feelings around your present post. Often these singularities present around people. You blame others for your bad mood.
Someone pays you a compliment.	You say, 'Thank you', and carry on feeling good about yourself.	You reply, 'I always look like this', and rush away in a huff. What did they mean by saying you look good! They didn't

		notice yesterday, did they!
You are walking down the street and someone you know is walking up the opposite street. You wave but they don't acknowledge you.	You think nothing of it. They were in their own world and didn't see you.	They're avoiding me! Now what did I do to get in their wrong books?

Table 2: Proactive v Reactive responses

The previous table is only representational but it does enough for the observer to realise that the more proactive your responses, the more you are actually opting for control in your life. Not only is this the better option, it feels it. Conversely, the more reactive responses in your life, the more you feel dumped on, avoided, ignored, passed over. Expats and non-expats alike exhibit proactive and reactive thinking. While thinking positively does not guarantee that you will open more doors of opportunity in your life automatically, thinking negatively will keep a multiplicity of doors closed. For some people, being miserable is an inverse happiness and they will attract more of the same into their lives. But the vast majority of expats and non-expats want to better themselves. They want to move forward in confidence. Whatever your experience as an expat it is likely to be replicated in your next posting unless you identify the thinking that is keeping you stuck and change the language you use to represent your life.

You hear the words you use. Are you earning a living then or living a life? You hear the words other people use. Are they earning a living or living a life? You are bombarded by self-chatter all the time. It is what your mind does. It is how it works. And most is deprecating, negative, and fearful. But you always have the choice to allow the fearful to dominate or to consciously choose new, positive thoughts.

Catch the expression, examine it, and make sure it works for you not against you. Take the first step today to get to the place where you are living a life while earning a living by changing how you think around the emotionally challenging situations that present in your life. You are always free to choose how you think in your own mind.

22

WORKING OR BEING WORKED

IN ALL MY journeys I have only encountered a handful of people who admit to being worked. Working abroad is perceived as the pinnacle of achievement by the expat, his or her family, and extended family. Being worked is rarely mentioned as it carries with it a hint of failure; of not being clever enough to see it coming, as being had. But it happens regularly. And it boxes you in. And it is harder to move on as those working you are the very people who will be writing your references. So you are caught.

> Whatever rung of the ladder you are on, once you recognise whether you are working or being worked, you have a choice.

You work harder while being increasingly disillusioned just so you can actually move on. The person or persons writing your reference can hold your life in their hands. It is a big trust issue to work for somebody you do not know. In **Chapter 21: Earning a living or living a life** discretionary choices were in your hands. Here, the choice trails are mixed; somebody else is directing you or yanking your chains. Your freedom of choice is impinged upon.

Working explains itself. It is a necessity; a way of exchanging brains or brawn, or both, for financial reward so you can earn a living or live a life. It can be a necessary money job or a planned career move that takes you abroad, into the unknown. The vast majority of people I have spoken to have worked for encouraging, supportive employers. They will work you too, of course, but it is within the terms of your contract, and these you know about and have accepted as a fair exchange. But sometimes in the course of a contract abroad the business morphs as it develops, and/or new management and leadership take over. These may or may not be as supportive as the old management or leadership. In fact, they rarely are, as the business has changed because something needs to be developed along slightly different lines or hugely different lines to continue to succeed. But they are likely to be supportive and encouraging along new lines and those who continue to thrive within the business are those who are most flexible and willing to learn.

Being worked can be an integral part of the work culture; never alluded to but widely practised. Or it can be delivered up front as when my husband and I turned up in Lagos, Nigeria and the Chairman of the Board said he would 'suck us dry' because he was paying us well. Some cultures that have a strong work culture see nothing wrong with 16-18 hour days. If you become immersed in such a work culture you may too busy keeping up that you will not have the time to consider what is actually happening in your life at all. Your Work Balance Wheel becomes your Life Balance Wheel. Being worked, alternatively, can be the outcome of a singularly driven CEO who cares about nothing else but the bottom line and drives those below him to deliver the goods whatever the cost. This cost has nothing to do with your take home pay which is unlikely to change whatever hours you put in as you have already agreed your pay beforehand. I have seen one instance where a new employee in a startup was not only expected to be on the job 24/7 but if there was a cash shortfall at the end of the month he was expected to contribute pro rata with the partners to make up the difference so the new company looked successful. He was not a partner. He was being cynically worked for the benefit of others. I cannot count the number of times I have heard stories about working the extra hours or being present at PR evening events that are not even acknowledged let alone remunerated. The company culture that has as its core 'working the employees' acts as if it owns them body and soul. And there is no Union to bail them out as expats.

This is an important point that expats need to understand: there is no Union of workers in the expat community to turn to for support. There are no strike options. However, in an understanding and professional business, there will be processes in place for discussion, performance review, and behavioural management. The ultimate control will be exercised by country authorities according to behavioural directives for foreigners. Breaching these, being caught with a local prostitute in China for example, will mean immediate deportation. As Barbara says earlier, live by your new country's rules and regulations whether you agree with them or not. You are only a guest. You are not a citizen. Global citizenship remains a term not a reality.

How can you recognise whether you are working or being worked? Working or being worked present differing characteristics that can be seen up front. This is a good starting point.

Characteristics of expat working can include:
- Advantageous pay for time spent
- Qualifications, expertise, continued learning taken into account
- Safe conditions
- Clear job description
- Agreed contract
- Agreed leave

- Performance reviews
- Grievance procedures
- Inflation-related pay reviews
- Housing consideration
- Health insurance
- Provision for children's schooling

Characteristics of expat being worked can include:
- Minimal pay
- Qualifications ignored
- Dodgy work conditions
- Vague job description
- Holding passport
- No performance reviews
- No grievance procedures
- No pay reviews
- Dormitory housing
- Basic health insurance, if any
- No provision for family or children
- Or it can include all the characteristics of working but you are

always on show, the useful expat ornament wheeled out as necessary. You are there to be seen to advise local counterparts where in reality this is in the realm of dreamland. The resistance to change is huge. As one local staff member articulated, 'You are the fifth Head I have seen come and go. I'm sure we'll survive the sixth as well.' The language used says it all! You will know you are being worked when your expertise is articulated but not acted upon, or worse still, your expertise is ignored.

There is an idea that the higher up the career ladder you go the less likely you are to be worked partly because you are more aware of the indicators and partly because no sane company would pay out a fortune for your expertise and then ignore you. While this may be truer in the regular business community, the expat community may experience it differently and this is partly culture based. Essentially, what you, as an expat, may perceive and know to be best practice in your business area, the foreign context may not be ready for all you have to offer straight up. They only want a small, sustainable percentage of your expertise and to grow it every year while you may want to go in guns blazing and revolutionise from the top down as soon as possible. Additionally, they may not understand what best practice is and the sooner you recognise this, the better, before you engender widespread resistance that defies improved sustainability long term. As an Executive, you may have to educate upwards to the Board as well as reform downwards to reach targets. If you are wise, you will work essentially as 'piggy in the middle' and let go of the limiting label of 'being worked'. That may be the unwritten culture but you are in a position to influence that. Give it a try. If it does not work, and you will know within six months, often six weeks, then you can plan a balanced exit without harming your onward career prospects or the business on the ground in its current sustainable form.

I have only once in my career seriously questioned my wisdom in upskilling the local staff. This was in Lagos. I had trained a number of very capable local staff in the new ICT system I had installed and we had enhanced this further with laptops for class use. It was a heady time of great improvement. I loved working with these intelligent, warm, enthusiastic staff, and the outcome on the ground was a win-win situation for everyone. But, in an impoverished society, so much hardware on the ground generated the worst kind of interest and we had an armed robbery in which one of our security staff was so badly beaten he was lucky to survive. 48 laptops were stolen. All my advice on security measures, and predictions of such an event up until then, were seemingly ignored. And so, once the horse had bolted, security measures were then put in place to keep him safely in his stall. Wounded pride at being burgled was obviously the ultimate incentive to put something in place that was needed from the beginning. People's lives were put at risk because of my improvement program and the Board's lack of urgency about what could happen. And they continued to be at risk but now there was an armed response unit which in itself acted as the ultimate deterrent. We replaced the laptops.

There is also an idea that younger expat staff can absorb being worked; that this is somehow a rite of passage that should not be avoided as it is character building. No doubt about it – it is indeed character building! But there is no guarantee that it is beneficially character building. Neither is there a guarantee that they will understand sufficiently the play that goes on behind the scene so they can separate out culture norms from greedy, narcissistic employers. There is also a chance that these young people will pay all this forward, becoming in their turn down the road, greedy, narcissistic employers themselves. Or they may become xenophobic, judging from the particular to the general. Or, in the best scenario, they may grow up a little and appreciate that there is no such thing as a free meal, and appreciate how good they were treated in a previous job. Every experience can provide a positive learning opportunity.

Whatever rung of the ladder you are on, once you recognise whether you are working or being worked, you have a choice. You can stay and learn from the experience or you can leave and learn from that experience. I always advise expat staff to keep to hand the necessary money for an exit should you find yourself in an unsustainable situation. If you do not have this money going into a position, make sure it is the first savings you make. And even before you take the job, find out if the company will 'keep' your passport until you finish your contract. Make the choice beforehand if you will be happy being 'stuck' for the duration. Sometimes all the money in the world is not worth the posting.

There are also identifiable differences in language associated with the phrases 'Working' or 'Being worked' which correlate to the above characteristics. I have illustrated these in Figures 7 and 8. These are used unconsciously and can offer you an insight into how you are thinking around work. They can also offer your employer, supervisor, and colleague the same insight into how you are thinking about work. And they can also offer you insight into how these same people are approaching work too. The good news is that once you are aware of these it helps you gain understanding of the workplace culture, country culture, or simply greedy, narcissistic managers or owners. A position of understanding is a position of power even if that power can only be wielded by you, on yourself. You remain, as always, the only one you can change. Even if you cannot change your circumstances for the better, you can change your response to rise above the situation. No one can take that from you.

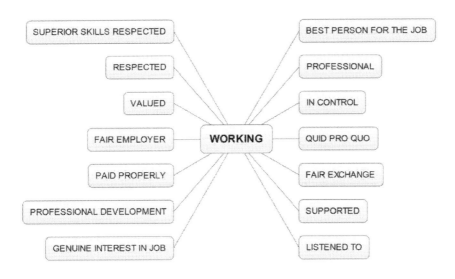

Figure 7: Working

Working is seen as a fair exchange; a positive exchange. It is how the world works. Some people attach a light label to working; others take it more seriously. Some have more of a focus on the outcome of work, the accumulation of wealth, which is more than the sheer monetary value accruing from a work/time investment. This is deeply personal. Others gain more from the altruistic opportunities that work allows. Some more place high value on teamwork and friendships within the workplace and are willing to weigh these elements alongside their salary; this is commonplace for both expat and non-expat workplaces but of a deeper intensity for the expat since the work pool is more curtailed. There is no one-best-fit for everyone. Your reasons to work, and stay in the workplace, or leave, are personal. The interesting thing is that the language used to describe your experience remains constant around the concept of working or being worked, whatever your reasons. Changing your language around working or being worked changes your personal experience.

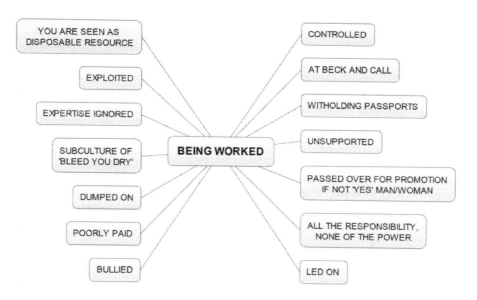

Figure 8: Being worked

There are clear cases of sweat shops that work their employees. Vulnerable people, illiterate people, migrants, to name a few, often find themselves being worked. They earn a subsistence wage and their living conditions are often appalling. They are doing the very best they can in an extremely difficult situation and are easily exploited. The lives of these people are often permeated by fear: fear of losing their job; of being homeless; of not being able to provide for their family. Fear walks the workplace too: fear of the boss or his minions; fear of not doing enough or of not doing it right; fear of reprisal. Nobody has the right to own somebody else yet that is exactly what these employers are doing. They work their employees to their own benefit.

While every workplace has its ups and downs, good days and bad, the overall experience needs to be respectful and professional. Each person brings more than their qualifications to the workplace. They bring their life experiences; their culture; their expectations; their hopes and aspirations; and their dreams. It is easy to see where misunderstandings around work may arise with so much diversity of life corralled in one place for eight hours, or more, a day. It is important to step back and check out your work balance regularly.

A Work Balance Wheel might include the following elements for you:

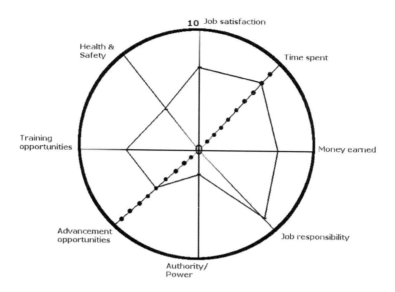

Figure 9: Work Balance Wheel

Check out your work balance right now:

- Draw a big circle
- Draw diagonals from the centre to the circumference for the areas you want to include in your life. Start with radials for Time spent, Money Earned, Job responsibility, Authority/Power, Advancement opportunities, Training opportunities, Health & Safety, and Job satisfaction. You can develop this more later. The size of the segments created is unimportant. The focus is on the radial.
- On each radial, measure off in equal increments from 0 at the centre to 10 at the circumference.

- Mark where you think you are along each radial, 0 being low satisfaction, 10 being total satisfaction.

- When you have done this for each radial/work element, join the dots. Ideally, what you are looking for is a smooth inside circle indicating all important areas of your work life are in synchronous balance. Usually what people find is that one or two areas are much closer to 0 or 10 than they realised. These are the priority areas to bring back into balance. Figure 9 is an example.

Knowing the reality of where you are in your work journey will help you identify underlying niggles and unease, and make it easier for you to articulate your findings to your superiors and find a way forward that works for you both. Additionally, it informs you of the way you want to go from here onwards. It identifies the depth of your feeling around the priorities you have listed. Your choices become clearer.

Occasionally the lines between working and being worked become fudged because of personal perceptions. These can include, but are not limited, to:

- The employee thinks they are better that they actually are
- The employee thinks they are doing better than they actually are
- The employer thinks the employee is better than they actually are
- The employer expects the employee to do better as a result.

Doing better often equates to doing more in the same timeframe or in less time and the employee ends up feeling squeezed, dumped on or worked, the employer unhappy with his progress. If the work is high profile the fallout will be greater. Comparisons with work colleagues can be unfavourably made. Good lines of communication can smooth the waters before things get out of hand. These are not 'being worked' situations; they are misunderstandings from both sides.

In the expat world I often hear the phrase, 'You can be a small fish in a big pond or a big fish in small pond'. When an expat takes her expertise to another country she is often alluded to as a 'big fish in a small pond'. If she remains at home she can be referred to as 'a small fish in a big pond'. The rarer the expertise exported, the larger the fish. And since all expats live the fishbowl existence, she will be noticed more as an expat than as a worker at home where the market can be saturated with similar expertise. Both expressions can carry negative and positive connotations. It is easier to move from being a small fish in a big pond to being a big fish in a small pond.

Fish size	Positivity	Negativity
Small fish in big pond	Job well done Additional training/learning	Invisibility complex Drowned out by competition More people with expertise lowers wages One of the boys
Big fish in small pond	Provide sustainable growth Accrue greater personal wealth Get noticed faster In a position of influence	Saviour complex Superiority No additional upskilling in situ Alone

Table 3: Fish in pond

Working or being worked can be both a physical reality and a personal perception. The language you use to describe your workday will assist you in identifying whether you are being worked or working. Your **Work Balance Wheel** will help you identify how you are doing in your job at any single point in time. Redo the exercise as often as you need. Learn from the words you say. Changing those words will make other people notice you differently. Because you choose to think differently you ARE different. And because you are different now the reality you experience will become different too, if not immediately, then in time.

23

OPPORTUNITY OF A LIFETIME OR HELL ON EARTH

I HAVE YET to meet a single expat who left home to work abroad for a hell on earth experience. Every single person I have talked to has left for an opportunity of bettering themselves and their families. Some of these opportunities have been offered; others have been achieved through the application and interview process. Every story starts with the excitement of the new opportunity. The vast majority of stories end with an additional expat move or a challenging repatriation. This Chapter: Opportunity of a Lifetime or Hell on Earth begins to look at what may be going on below the surface. **Expat Life: Carousel Moves,** begins where this chapter ends and delves into the reasons for, and experiences of, expats who continue to move from country to country during their working lives. What is going on when the opportunity of a lifetime can tip into hell on earth?

> It is often the small things, the petty irritants that create the tipping point from opportunity of a lifetime to hell on earth.

Overseas opportunities are very exciting. They have a similarity in finding your dream job at home with the added excitement of travelling and living abroad. They are validating beyond the home culture job because somebody foreign has recognised your worth, maybe more than anyone at home has. You look forward to meeting exciting new people, world people. You find their thinking refreshing; their living and work ways enchanting and positively challenging. You live the dream. And that is where you need to begin. Where you wake up from the dream and try to make sense of the new reality. You have moved away from your old life; you have moved towards your new life; and now you are living a different life. It is not new anymore. It is like buying a new pair of shoes: with use, the shine wears off a little and your feet may be a little sore as you break them in. Question is: will they ever be a best fit? Or will they ever fit you properly? And even more basically, will you continue to like the look of them?

There are a lot of positive emotions around an opportunity to live and work overseas as an expat. What has taken you thus far is your strength of character, your attitude to life, your expectations of life, your qualifications, and your determination to succeed. Your personal perceptions of your life, as it now is, are your basis of comparison for your future one. And personal perceptions ride the wave of your emotional state with impunity. It is very possible to be blinded by opportunity. From where you stand, everything looks rosy and you cannot wait to get going. This is a very common response to achieving a job overseas. Your success in your move will be based on all these factors plus how much preparation you have made beforehand and whether you will continue to have a glass half full mentality when the learning curves are steep.

The language around an 'opportunity of a lifetime' mentality is extremely positive. It is upbeat, exciting, and catching. You will attract people to your inner circle who speak the same language as you. You will feed off each other's excitement and the honeymoon settling in period can last way into the future as you support and encourage each other along. You may well continue to speak the same language from positive habit when the first challenges in your different life present themselves. You may continue through thick and thin to present the same upbeat, excited profile in your determination to see your entire move through positively. You may even deny that elements in your life are niggling you; that all is not as rosy as you first thought. You may not be able to let yourself believe that your first impressions were not correct as this may point to poor judgement, and if you let go, what will this mean about subsequent moves. There is absolutely nothing wrong with rosy first impressions. In fact, there is everything right with them. They allow you the comfort of seeing a huge transition through more easily. It engenders a positivity about your job and environment that will help you through those initial steep learning curves. But if you continue to define reality as rosy all the time you lose the opportunity to learn, to develop new understandings of your new culture, friends, and environment. It is not the challenges you meet along the way that defines you; it is how you respond to those challenges that makes the learning difference. Let yourself see with new eyes; with new understanding from your immersion with new foreigners and new cultures. Living as an expat reveals just as much about your home culture and your programmed cultural responses as it does about new cultures and differing cultural responses. Listen to the words you use to describe your new opportunity. Eventually some of the words from Figure 11: Hell on Earth will mingle with words from Figure 10: Opportunity of a Lifetime. These may be used to describe petty irritants. These petty irritants may go on to become deal breakers. Constant use of Hell on Earth language will alert you to your unhappiness and lack of fulfilment in a post. Your goal is to avoid this continuous state. Your work is to manage its occasional appearance as you progress through life.

MAKING GOOD PROGRESS

UPBEAT

GOING PLACES

POSITIVITY

UPSKILLING

FEEL GOOD FACTOR

PROFESSIONAL

SELF WORTH

BALANCE

OPPORTUNITY OF A LIFETIME

IMPROVEMENT IN ALL DESIRED AREAS/ ALL AREAS

CONTENT

GLASS HALF FULL

RESPECTED

HAPPY

INCREASING INFLUENCE

EXCITING

LIFE PLAN

ENTHUSIASM

Figure 10: Opportunity of a lifetime

It is often the small things, the petty irritants that create the tipping point from opportunity of a lifetime to hell on earth. The big changes, the big things, take the vast majority of your strength and reserve. These you have expected, somewhat. Proportionately, you may be a little off balance with the big things, as you put them out there to be dealt with first. Among those big things are your new job, your financial situation, and your health. They are right in front of you; it is impossible to ignore them. The small things creep up on you however. You rarely see them coming. And your responses are not pre-prepared. Those little things can include:

- Surprising or unexpected job element changes
- Unexpected environmental irritants – mosquitoes, cockroaches, noise pollution, stairs/steps, spitting, etc.
- Unacceptable cultural habits (from your cultural perception)
- Toxic peers
- Loneliness
- Lack of love interest

- Betrayal
- Physical danger
- Anything unexpected and unwelcome that catches you on the hop

FEELING 'HAD'

ILLNESS

NO UPSKILLING

ANXIETY

GLASS HALF FULL — **HELL ON EARTH**

BLACKMAILED BY BOSS

GOING NOWHERE

PASSPORT HELD

OVERWEIGHT/UNDERWEIGHT

CIRCUMSTANCES OUTSIDE CONTROL

PUT UPON

NEGATIVITY

STRESS

NOT RESPECTED

WORKING BENEATH CAPACITY

DEPRESSION

TRAPPED

RESTRICTED CHOICES

Figure 11: Hell on Earth

Very small irritants can punch above their weight and tip your emotional balance into negativity. There is a certain naivety in moving abroad that everyone will be as altruistic as you are, for instance. Nothing is further from the truth. You find the same range of personalities and problems as experienced at home except that in an expat conclave it is harder to find alternative people to socialise with initially. With working peers you have to learn how to get along. Awkward people may pollute your dream experience. You may have to dig deep to rise above it all. And eventually it may be a deal breaker.

Working and living as an expat has recognisable highs and lows. The first high is with the job offer and the subsequent move. The first low can be as early as six weeks in. You have created new cultural and living habits in that time and your subconscious intervenes to check if you really want to put all this new stuff into habit. This is not a 'hell on earth' moment but it does present negatively, throwing your new life into stark contrast with your previous comfort zone. You may suddenly feel trapped or anxious in your new environment. You may be dismayed that all your new learning and adapting has been for nothing. You may be intensely homesick although you have not missed home once since you arrived. This pattern may present several times along your new journey but each episode will be less intense. And once you know it is just the process of new habit forming you can settle back into control of your life within minutes.

True hell on earth experiences do not present with highs and lows that are easily managed once you recognise the habit forming process. True hell on earth experiences are characterised by the following, to name a few:

- Constant high anxiety states
- Fearfulness
- Withdrawing from society
- Depression
- Isolation, often by choice
- Feeling of lack of control in all circumstances
- Emotional numbness
- Stuckness
- Illnesses
- Addictions
- Excesses – smoking, drinking, drugs, eating, etc.

Many expats have experienced a lingering of elements within this list. Some have come to believe that this is what expat living is all about, the mingling of the opportunity of a lifetime with hell on earth, that this is expat reality. And to some degree this is true. There is no perfect posting abroad or anywhere else. But some present this belief as a means of relaxing into learned behaviour or responses that do not serve them well. They allow their perceptions to become fixed and they continue to live in their current posting with a jaundiced view of reality or they move on and take the same view with them. And then they cannot understand why history repeats itself, why they end up with the same experience in every move.

Listen to the language you are using to describe your current situation. Identify where your thought processes are taking you. If you are happy with where you are, that is great. If not, which language descriptions are keeping you embroiled in negativity? Once you identify what you are really putting out there into the world about your life you are a position of informed clarity. Change your thinking around the situation or not; the choice is yours.

A final thought – maybe the change really needs to start with you. Maybe it is you that is intransigent, confused, and mixed up. Maybe you are more part of the problem than you realised. If you find yourself describing those around you in negative terms with each move, this says more about you than those you describe. In the end, the only one you get to change is you. The ball is firmly in your court. How comfortable have you made those shoes? Maybe it is time for a new pair.

As Albert Einstein once said, 'insanity is doing the same thing over and over again and expecting different results.'

24

EPILOGUE: HOW AM I DOING

It took me a long time to realise the importance of understanding my own personality strengths and needs in living as an expat. I am a quiet, solitary person much like the character Alice in Chapter 13: Job Matters. I need time to personalise details, to see the bigger picture, to make sure nothing is left to chance. I like to make sure everyone is taken care of. I see where, with a little more thought and consideration, things can be improved, often so easily that it frustrates me that others don't see it. I often lead with this, and this frustrates others. In working through a project I am a perfectionist. It is important to me to get things right, first time. In this, I am like Ann in Chapter 13. I need the details to be right, for everyone.

In my personal life I need solitude to recharge or quality time with a few good friends. I am happy with a good book, one I can learn from. I am content being alone for long stretches. I love silence, the sound of birds singing, the seaside, and rushing water in a brook. I admire quality, a beautiful piece of art, a tranquil piece of music. A measured, regular pace of live sees me through the bulk of my work but I relish the new, the creative, and I can become immersed in it to the exclusion of all else.

Expat life hit me with a huge social impact. All the newness at once was very draining. Most of this came from people who felt to help me settle in they had to invade my reserve. I needed to adapt to their way, instantly. Come on down the pub. The social work gatherings that was fantastic for someone who thrived on those events. The go, go, go of constant investigation, sightseeing, socialising. Everything was new. Everyone was new. And I was expected to become one of the gang. Now don't get me wrong, these were very hospitable, generous people. They wanted to make sure I wasn't lonely. But my quiet self was blinded by it all. I was more exhausted from these people interactions than the work, the environment, and the local culture put together. My emotions were engaged constantly. I couldn't let these people down. I needed to be seen as one of the gang to fit in asap.

With the exhaustion and excitement it took longer than usual to identify the dynamics that were in place. There were 'interest' groups with their own agendas; cliques, if you will, that thrived on news and stories of the day. Higher status was accorded those that could have the most up-to-date information on what was going to happen next at work; who was going out with who; who dropped the ball significantly. Back home, they would be called a bunch of dangerous gossips. Here, they were almost all that was available for socialising with.

Bit by bit, I identified the Matthews, again from Chapter 13: Job Matters; the ones who were either truly extrovert and couldn't help themselves or those who had made a career of proposing ideas up front, of shooting their mouths off, and then leaving others to pick up the pieces. They could never be fully ignored as they really did come up with some excellent ideas; they were 'outside the box' thinkers in so many ways.

The Gregs were a law unto themselves. Great workers when pointed in the right direction but don't ask them to change mid-stream. They are so dependable. They'll be exactly where they said they would be, doing exactly what they said they would be doing.

I learned so much from all these people in my closed expat working and living situation. Somehow, being so insulated from the totality of the local culture helped me see the strengths that people were working from more easily. I needed to learn how I, and others, worked to understand how to integrate my strengths with theirs. I needed to learn how I, and other expats, socialised to understand what drained me or what empowered me in this expat posting. Understanding these two major points of possible people clashes gave me choice as to how to best work and integrate socially. Inside these possible people clashes I needed to further understand whether there were cultural differences at play, gender issues or just plain personality differences. Learning to identify the difference between salt and sugar seems so much weak beer by comparison.

Working and living as an expat brings change to your door. After a while, when the change strangeness is conquered, what is left can seem mundane. This happens more quickly if your move is within Europe as opposed to within Asia, for example, depending on your nationality. While, of necessity, I focussed initially on the physical strangeness of moving to Tokyo to get settled in, the change involved in understanding people and cultural change went on behind the scenes. After all, I couldn't buy tea bags from the supermarket without interacting with local staff. Myself, my character, my personality was dealing with all that as if on auto pilot. The person I was when I went to Tokyo took on new living within the strengths and weakness I brought with me. I was really glad I had spent some time reading up on what local people thought respectful before I reached their shores.

I am still thrilled with all of my expat journeys. I have learned so much about who I am and what, of real worth, I can offer the world.

I am not perfect. My journeys were not always trouble-free. I made mistakes along the way. I made great choices and poor choices. In this, I am like anyone else, anywhere. I am one human among many humans.

"Character is a journey, not a destination."
William J Clinton

ABOUT THE AUTHOR

Geraldine Donnellan is an NLP life coach and teacher. An expat since 1989, she has worked and lived in Dublin, Ireland; London, UK; Tokyo, Japan; Prague, Czech Republic; Lagos, Nigeria; Shanghai, PR China; and Florence, Italy where she now lives with her husband and best friend of thirty eight years. She is the mother of two, both living the expat life with international partners. Her grandchildren are coming to know the world is a small place indeed. Experiencing differentness is normal to them.

Geraldine is CEO of Gallan & Amral Enterprises Ltd, a company she and her husband set up to promote education, information and learning. She has written many articles on life coaching and alternative health, some of which are available on her website. Her first novel, The Greenway Conspiracy, Book 1 in the Symphony of Time, was published in 2013, and is available on Amazon and in other outlets.

Contact Geraldine through www.gallanamral.com or by direct email at geraldine@gallanamral.com

Made in the USA
Charleston, SC
01 February 2016